A To Z of Internet

by
Bittu Kumar

Published by:

F-2/16, Ansari Road, Daryaganj, New Delhi-110002
☎ 011-23240026, 011-23240027 • *Fax:* 011-23240028
Email: info@vspublishers.com • *Website:* www.vspublishers.com

Branch : Hyderabad
5-1-707/1, Brij Bhawan (Beside Central Bank of India Lane)
Bank Street, Koti, Hyderabad - 500 095
☎ 040-24737290
E-mail: vspublishershyd@gmail.com

Branch Office : Mumbai
Jaywant Industrial Estate, 2nd Floor–222, Tardeo Road
Opposite Sobo Central Mall, Mumbai – 400 034
☎ 022-23510736
E-mail: vspublishersmum@gmail.com

Follow us on:

All books available at **www.vspublishers.com**

© Copyright: *V&S Publishers*
Edition 2017

The Copyright of this book, as well as all matter contained herein (including illustrations) rests with the Publishers. No person shall copy the name of the book, its title design, matter and illustrations in any form and in any language, totally or partially or in any distorted form. Anybody doing so shall face legal action and will be responsible for damages.

Printed at Repro Knowledgecast Limited, Thane

Contents

- Chapter 1 – Networking and Basics of Internet 5
  - Exploring Your Networking Options 5
  - Wireless 5
  - Ethernet 6
  - HomePNA 6
  - Powerline 6
  - Hybrid 7
  - Networking Hardware Checklist 7
  - Wireless Networking Hardware 7
  - Setting Up Your Network 7
    - Installing the Hardware 7
    - Setting Up Your Internet Connection 8
    - Connecting the Cables and Cords 8
    - Connecting a Printer 8
    - Turning Everything On 9
    - Setting Up a Wireless Router 9
    - Running the Set Up a Network Wizard 10
    - Choosing a Network Location 10
    - Testing Your Network 11
  - Creating a Homegroup 12
    - Joining a Homegroup 13
    - Sharing Files in a Homegroup 13
    - Checking an Item's Share Setting 14
    - Accessing Shared Disks, Folders, and Files 14
  - Printer 14
    - Installing a Printer on Your Network 14
    - Installing a Network Printer 15
    - Sharing a Printer 15
  - Securing Your Network 16
- Chapter 2 – Disk Operating System (DOS) 17
  - Brief introduction to DOS and its need 17
    - Getting Started with DOS 17
    - Starting and Working with DOS in Windows 7 18
    - DOS Commands 'cd\,' 'time,' 'date,' and 'cls' 18
    - Acquiring Elevated or Administrative Privileges 20
    - Changing Current file type 21
    - Creating a File Using the DOS Command 'copy con filename,' 21
    - Using the DOS Commands 'type,' 'ren,' and 'del' 22
- Chapter 3 – Getting Wired to the Internet 25
  - Understanding How Internet Works 25
  - Picking a Connection Type 25
  - Turbo-Charging Your Connection with a Cable Modem 26
  - Another Speedy Option: DSL 26
  - Connecting from the Boonies via Satellite 26
  - On the Go with Wireless Internet 27
  - Chugging Along with Dial-Up 28
  - Shopping for an Internet Service Provider 28
  - Establishing a Connection 28
  - Testing Your Connection Speed 29
  - Poking Around on the World Wide Web 30
  - Browsing for a Web Browser 30
  - Steering Your Browser in the Right Direction 30
  - A Word about Web Page Addresses 31
  - Finding Stuff with Google and Other Search Tools 31
  - Locating People Online 32
  - Navigating Multiple Pages with Tabs 32
  - Going Back in Time with the History List 33
  - Marking Your Favourite Web Pages 33
  - Changing the Starting Web Page 34
- Chapter 4 – Google Search, Email and more 35
  - Performing a Basic Search 35
  - Focusing on Specific Content 36
  - Performing an Advanced Search 36
  - Browsing the Website Directory 36
  - Adjusting Your Search Settings 36
  - Cool Google Search Tips and Tricks 37
  - Creating a Google Account 38
    - Feature Website Address 38
  - Checking Out Other Search Sites and Tools 38
  - Sending and Receiving E-Mail 39
  - Using an E-Mail Program 39
  - Setting Up Your Account 39
  - Addressing an Outgoing Message 40
  - Checking Your E-Mail 41
  - Sending Replies 41
  - Adding Photos and Other Cool Stuff 41
  - Attaching Documents to Your Messages 42
    - DEFINITION 42
  - What About Free, Web-Based E-Mail? 43
  - Emoticons and E-Mail Shorthand 43
    - Emoticon Meaning 43
    - Abbreviation Meaning 44
    - Abbreviation Meaning 44
    - E-Mail No-No's 45
- Chapter 5 – You Tube 46
  - Searching and Browsing on YouTube 46
  - Searching for Specific Video Footage 46
  - Browsing YouTube's Video Collection 47
  - Doing more through a YouTube Account 47
  - Creating an Account 47
  - Signing In and Signing Out 48
  - Saving Your Favourites 48
  - Creating Additional Playlists 48
  - Subscribing to a Channel 48
  - Sharing a Video with Others 49

- Rating and Commenting on Videos 49
- Sharing Your Videos 50
- Prepping a Video for Uploading 50
- Uploading Your Video to YouTube 50
- Recording a Video with a Webcam 51
- Getting Help 51

Chapter 6 – Twitter 52
- Creating a Twitter Account 52
- Signing In and Signing Out 53
- Fleshing Out Your Profile 53
- Tweaking Your Account Settings 53
- Reading and Replying to Tweets 53
- Reading a Tweet 53
- Replying to a Tweet and Retweeting 54
- Flagging a Tweet as a Favourite 55
- Posting Tweets 55
- Adding a Link 55
- Deleting a Tweet 55
- Following Users on Twitter 56
- Searching for People on Twitter 56
- Seeing Who's Following You 56
- Exchanging Direct Messages in Private 56
- Learning More About Twitter 57

Chapter 7 – Communicating One-on-One in Real Time 58
- Instant Messaging with AIM 58
- Getting Started with AIM 58
- Building a Buddy List 59
- Instant Messaging 59
- Audio Instant Messaging 60
- Video Instant Messaging 60
- Texting a Buddy's Mobile Phone 60
- Getting AIM for Your Cellphone 60
- Sampling Other Chat/Instant Messaging Clients 61
- Placing Really Cheap (or Free) Phone Calls with Skype ... 61
- Getting Skype 62
- Adding Contacts 62
- Making Free Skype-to-Skype Calls 62
- Cheap Long Distance with PC-to-Phone Calls 64

Chapter 8 – Saving and Making Money Online 65
- Is It Safe? 65
- Comparison-Shopping for the Real Deals 66
- Buying Online 66
- Booking Travel Reservations Online 67
- Buying and Selling on eBay 68
- Buying Stuff on eBay 69
- Selling Stuff on eBay 71

Chapter 9 – Blogs & Web Page 72
- Behind the Scenes with a Web Page 72
- Forget About HTML 72
- Creating a Free Website with Google Sites 73
- Editing Your Google Site 74
- Inserting Objects and Apps 75
- Inserting Gadgets 75
- Saving or Cancelling Your Changes 76
- Blogging Your Way to Internet Fame 76
- Definition 76
- Launching Your Blog 76
- Making Your Own Blog 78
- Embedding a YouTube Video in a Web Page or Blog Post 78

Chapter 10 – Internet Safety 80
- Keeping Out Viruses and Other Malware 80
- Detecting and Eliminating Spyware 81
- Keeping Hackers at Bay with a Firewall 81
- Configuring Your Router's Firewall 82
- Limiting Access to Your Wireless Network 82
- Activating or Deactivating the Windows Firewall 82
- Making Exceptions for Certain Programs 83
- Securing Your Portable PC in Public Hot Spots 83
- Updating Windows 7 84
- Opting for a Standard User Account 85
- Dealing with E-Mail Threats and Annoyances 85
- Avoiding Infected E-Mail Attachments 85
- Don't Even Preview Junk Mail 85
- Avoiding Phishing Scams 86
- Avoiding, Filtering, and Blocking Spam 87
- Checking Your Browser's Security Settings 87

Chapter 1

Networking and Basics of Internet

People generally network their PCs for two reasons:

- To share files and other resources, including a printer, a high-speed Internet connection, and a backup drive among two or more computers, to establish a connection with a *Wi-Fi hotspot*. A *hotspot* is a location that offers a wireless network connection for connecting to the Internet. You're likely to find hotspots in coffee shops, hotels and motels, and airports.

- To allow friends, roommates, or family members to play multiuser games. In this chapter, you discover the four most common ways to network computers, how to use the Windows networking features to set up a network and share files and resources, and how to connect to a Wi-Fi hotspot when you're on the road with your PC.

Exploring Your Networking Options

When planning your network, the first step is to decide which type of networking hardware you want to use. The following sections discuss your options and some important considerations for making the best choice for your situation and needs. The costs involved are comparable for each option.

Wireless

Wi-Fi networks enable computers to communicate via radio waves. The biggest advantages of wireless are that you can set up a network without having run cables, and you can move the computers almost anywhere in your home or office without losing your connection. The three main drawbacks are that wireless is generally slower than the other three options; Wi-Fi networks are less secure (because data is transmitted through airwaves); and signal interference can be caused by walls, pipes, electrical wiring, cordless phones, and microwave ovens. Still, Wi-Fi is almost always the most attractive choice for most homes and small businesses.

Note....

Some Wi-Fi signals can reach pretty far—150 to 350 feet—so be sure to secure your network to keep unauthorized users (such as your neighbours) from accessing your data or using your broadband Internet service Wi-Fi data transfer rates vary depending on the standard, as you'll see later. A maximum data transfer rate (under ideal conditions) of 54 megabits per second (Mbps) is pretty standard. At that rate, it takes about 1.5 seconds to download a 10MB file. The newest Wi-Fi standard can transfer data at speeds up to 600Mbps under ideal conditions.

Ethernet

Fast, reliable, secure, and inexpensive, Ethernet networks are an excellent choice if all your computers are in one room or you don't mind running network cables throughout your home or business.

Ethernet networks have data transfer rates of 10, 100, or 1,000Mbps, depending on the type of cables. Transferring a 10MB file over a 100Mbps connection takes about 1 second.

Ethernet

HomePNA

Secure and potentially inexpensive, Home Phoneline Networking Alliance (HomePNA) enables you to network computers over existing phone lines. HomePNA 2.0 is relatively slow, with a data transfer rate of 10Mbps—about the same speed as a slow wireless network. HomePNA 3.0 features data transfer rates of up to 128Mbps—about double the speed of most wireless networks.

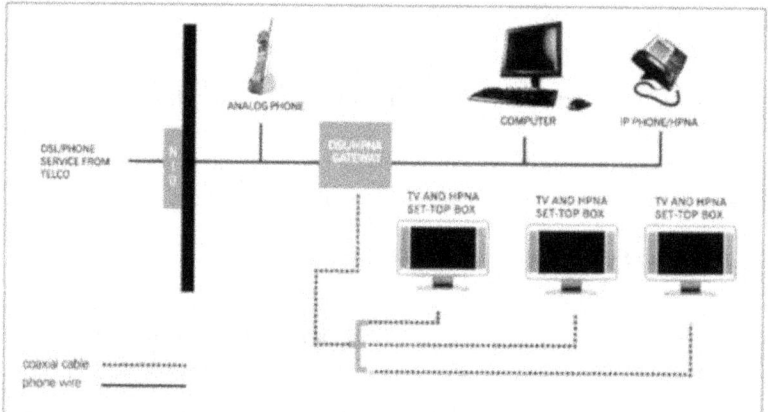
Home PNA

Powerline

Fast (up to 200Mbps), reliable, secure, and inexpensive, Powerline networking enables you to connect computers using existing electrical wiring in your home or business. The main drawback of powerline networks is that electrical "noise" on the line can interfere with the signal.

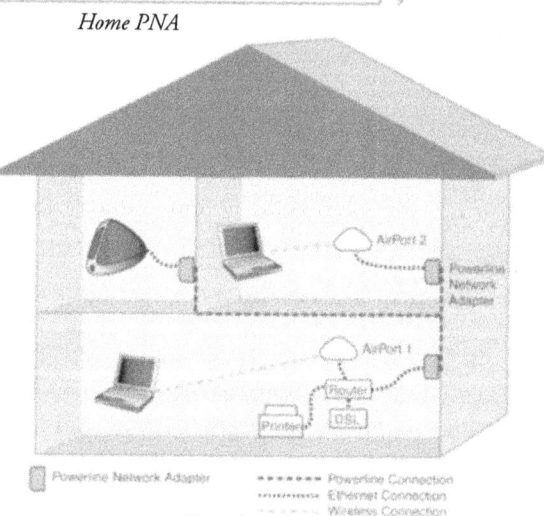
Powerline

Hybrid

You can combine the networking technologies discussed here to create a hybrid network. For example, you can build an Ethernet network that connects all the computers in your office and then use a wireless or phone line.

Networking Hardware Checklist

Chances are good that if the computers you plan to network are relatively new, some or all of them have a LAN port (for an Ethernet network) or some sort of Wi-Fi capability. Knowing which hardware you already have on hand may influence your choice of networking configuration. In the following sections, you take inventory of the hardware you already have and determine which hardware you need for each of your networking options.

Wireless Networking Hardware

To set up a wireless network, you need two things:

- **Wireless router or access point:** A *wireless router* is best and essential if you plan to share an Internet connection, because it can assign an Internet address to each networked computer and provides a more secure connection between your network and the Internet. An *access point* merely enables two or more computers to connect with one another. (Most wireless routers have several LAN ports on the back as well, for hardwiring computers and other devices to the network.)
- **Wireless adapters:** Every computer must have a wireless networking adapter or built-in Wi-Fi support that's compatible with the router. (Compatibility is a function of the frequency the devices use to communicate: 2.4GHz or 5GHz.) Almost all portable PCs have a built-in wireless adapter.
- Determining whether a PC already has a wireless networking adapter is pretty easy. Click **Start**, **Control Panel**, **Hardware and Sound**, **Device Manager**. Click the arrow to the left of Network adapters and look for an entry that includes "Wireless Network Adapter." Unfortunately, determining the standard(s) the adapter supports is not so easy. Check your PC's documentation or the box it came in, contact the manufacturer, or search for the make and model online.

Setting Up Your Network

After you've decided on the type of network you want and gathered the requisite hardware, you're ready to set up your network, as explained in the following sections.

Installing the Hardware

Following the manufacturer's instructions, install or connect a network adapter to every computer that doesn't already have one. See Chapter 10 for more information about installing new hardware devices. If you're going to use a wireless router, choose a location and position it in a way to reduce potential interference:

- Choose a central location. If you're going to be using computers all over your home or office, position the router as close to centre as possible. If you're using computers in only a portion of your home or office, choose the centre location in that portion.

- ❏ Reduce potential obstructions. Choose a location off the floor and away from walls, metal filing cabinets, and anything else that might block the signal.
- ❏ Reduce potential interference. Position your router away from microwave ovens and the most common areas where you use a cordless phone, if possible. Networking equipment that uses a 5GHz frequency can help reduce interference from cordless phones and microwaves. 802.11a and 802.11n devices are less susceptible. If your network primarily uses 802.11g (2.4GHz) networking equipment, shop for phones and other devices that operate at a higher frequency, such as 5.8GHz.

Setting Up Your Internet Connection

If you plan to share an Internet connection, now is a good time to set it up. Chances are pretty good that if you have high-speed Internet service, your service provider sent a technician to set up the modem on one of your computers and establish the connection for you. All you have to do is disconnect the modem's cable from the PC and plug it into the designated Internet port on the back of the router—the port is typically labeled "Internet," "WAN" (wide area network), or "WLAN" (wireless local area network). Some services supply a combination modem/router, which makes your job even easier—just plug the device into the designated port on any of your networked computers.

Connecting the Cables and Cords

The process for connecting the computers and other devices on your network varies, depending on the type of network.

Make the following connections based on your network configuration:

- ❏ **Wireless:** Plug the wireless router into your surge protector.
- ❏ **Ethernet:** Connect the Ethernet cable from each computer's LAN port to the router, hub, or switch, and then plug the router, hub, or switch into your surge protector.
- ❏ **HomePNA:** Using standard telephone cables, connect each computer's HomePNA network adapter to a phone jack.
- ❏ **Powerline:** Plug each computer's Powerline adapter into an electrical outlet.

Connecting a Printer

Now you should have everything connected except, perhaps, the printer. This varies based on the type of printer you have and how you want to connect it:

Network printer, wired: If your printer has a LAN port, you can connect it to the router. All computers on the network can then use the printer independently through the router.

Network printer, wireless: This printer is similar to a wired network printer, but it connects to the network through the wireless router. (Some wireless network printers also include a LAN port.)

USB printer: Connect the printer to a USB port on the computer from which you'll do most of your printing. The other computers can then access the printer through this computer. The only drawback is that the computer attached to the printer must be turned on for the other computers to use it.

Bluetooth printer: If all your networked computers are Bluetooth enabled and within range, they can connect to the printer independently. Otherwise, the computer must connect to the printer through one of the Bluetooth enabled computers.

Turning Everything On

In certain cases, you can turn on all the computers and the modem, printer, router, and other devices in any sequence, and everything works fine. Sometimes, however, something doesn't work—for example, if you turn on the computer and router before turning on the modem, the modem may have trouble establishing an Internet connection.

The proper sequence for powering up your network is to work from the outside (peripherals) back to the computer:

- Turn on the modem and wait for the lights to indicate that the modem has established a connection.
- Turn on the router and wait about 30 seconds for it to detect the modem.
- Turn on the computer you want to use.

If you're setting up a wired network (Ethernet, HomePNA, or Powerline), all computers on the network that are turned on should be connected, but you may still need to set up your router to establish an Internet connection. Check the installation instructions included with your router. Setting up a wireless network is more involved, as explained in the following section

Setting Up a Wireless Router

Most routers include a setup disc. After turning on the router and at least one of the computers on the network, insert the disc into one of the computers that's up and running. Windows should automatically launch the router setup routine from the disc. If it doesn't, find the Setup or Install file on the disc and double-click it. The steps for setting up a router for the first time vary depending on the router and the manufacturer's setup routine. However, they all require that you do the following:

- Establish an Internet connection. Because all of your computers will connect to the Internet through the router, you may need to provide the router with the username and password your ISP has assigned to you.
- Give your network a name. Most routers initially use a default network name, but for security purposes, assigning a unique name is a good idea. Network names are case sensitive, and every computer on the network needs to use the same network name to connect.
- Choose an encryption level, such as WiFi Protected Access (WPA) or WPA-2. This secures the network by blocking unauthorized access and encrypting data as it flows through the network.
- Specify a passphrase (password). A secure passphrase includes a mix of upper- and lowercase letters, numbers, and symbols (-, _, &, $, and so on). Initially, all computers on your network will use the same passphrase.

Write down the network name, encryption level, and passphrase, because you'll need to enter this information on all of the computers you want to include in the network.

Running the Set Up a Network Wizard

Running the Set Up a Network Wizard If your router did not include a disc, you can use Windows to set up your network. Windows features a Set Up a Network Wizard that leads you step by step through the process of configuring all computers on your wireless network to establish a connection with the network:

- ❏ Click Start, Control Panel to display the Control Panel.
- ❏ Click Network and Internet and then Network and Sharing Centre.
- ❏ Below Network and Sharing Centre, click Set up a new connection or network.
- ❏ Click Set up a new network, and then follow the wizard's instructions to set up your network.

The Set Up a Network Wizard can save the network settings to a USB drive to make it easier to add other computers to the network. You can then insert the USB drive into another computer and, in the AutoPlay dialog box, select Wireless Network Setup Wizard to have Windows automatically configure the computer to connect to the network. Otherwise, take the following steps to add another computer to the network:

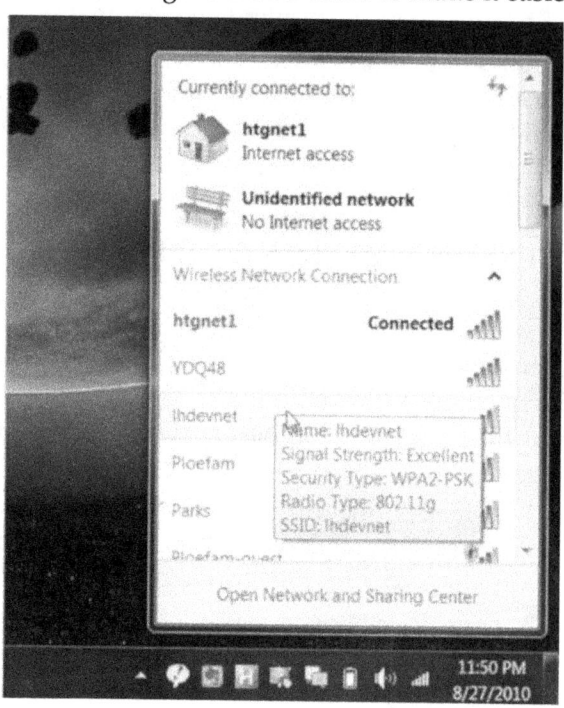

- ❏ Click Start, Control Panel, Network and Internet.
- ❏ Below Network and Sharing Centre, click Connect to a network.
- ❏ Click the wireless network from the list that appears and click Connect, as shown in Figure.
- ❏ Follow the onscreen instructions to enter whatever information is required, such as the network name, encryption level, or passphrase/security key.

Setting up a network wizard

Choosing a Network Location

Networking computers increases their exposure to unauthorized access and to malware (viruses, spyware, and so on), especially if the computers share an Internet connection. The risk level varies depending on the network. A home network is relatively safe, whereas a Wi-Fi hotspot outside your home poses a greater risk. Whenever you connect to a network for the first time, Windows prompts you to choose a network location, which contains security settings appropriate for the type of network you're connecting to. To choose a network location, click **Start, Control Panel, Network and Internet, Network and Sharing Centre**.

Below View your active networks, click your current network location (**Home**, **Work**, or **Public**) and then choose the desired location:

- **Home network:** On a home network, you know all the networked computers and users, so Windows can let down its guard. Computers on a home network can join a homegroup, and network discovery is turned on, so networked computers and devices can identify one another and access shared resources.

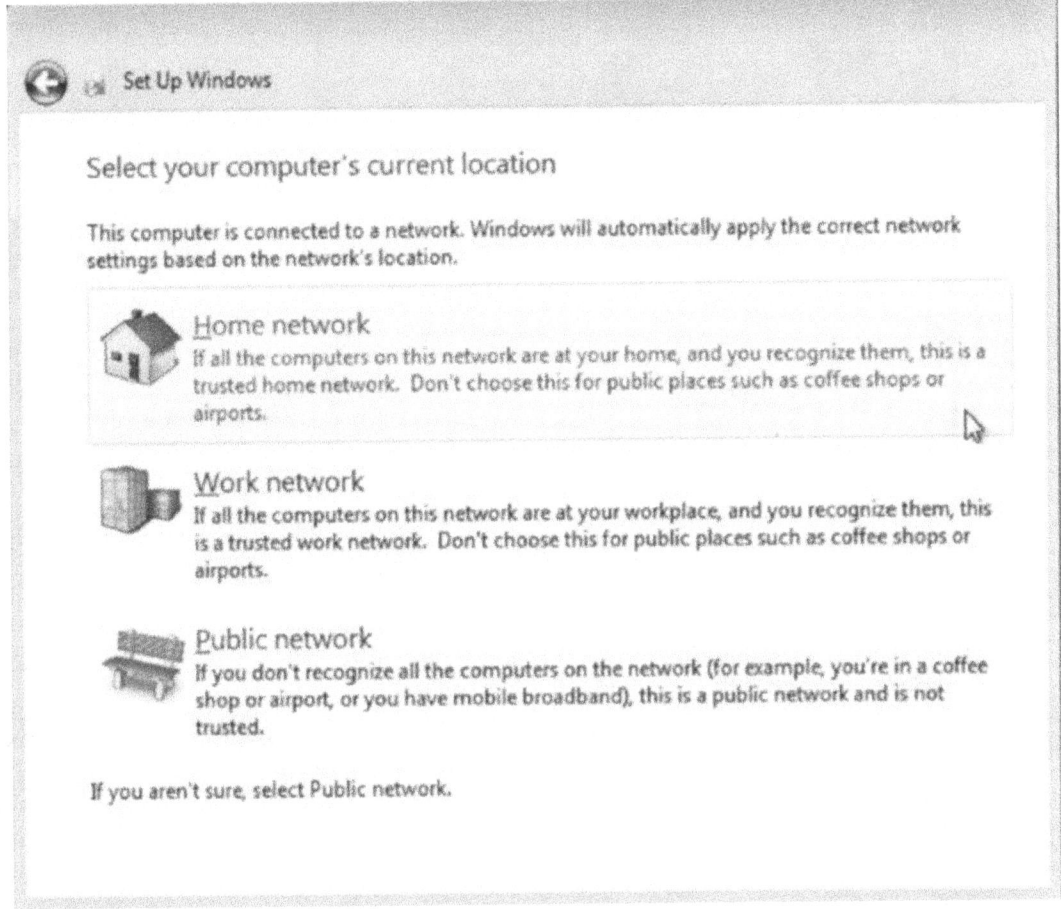

- **Work network:** Network discovery is enabled, so networked computers can see shared resources on your computer and vice versa, but you can't create or join a homegroup.
- **Public network:** This option attempts to keep your PC and any shared resources invisible and inaccessible when connecting in a public place, such as a coffee shop, or connecting directly to the Internet without the protection of a router.

Testing Your Network

To test your network, make sure everything is turned on, and then click **Start**, **Computer**, **Network**. You should see an icon for every computer on the network.

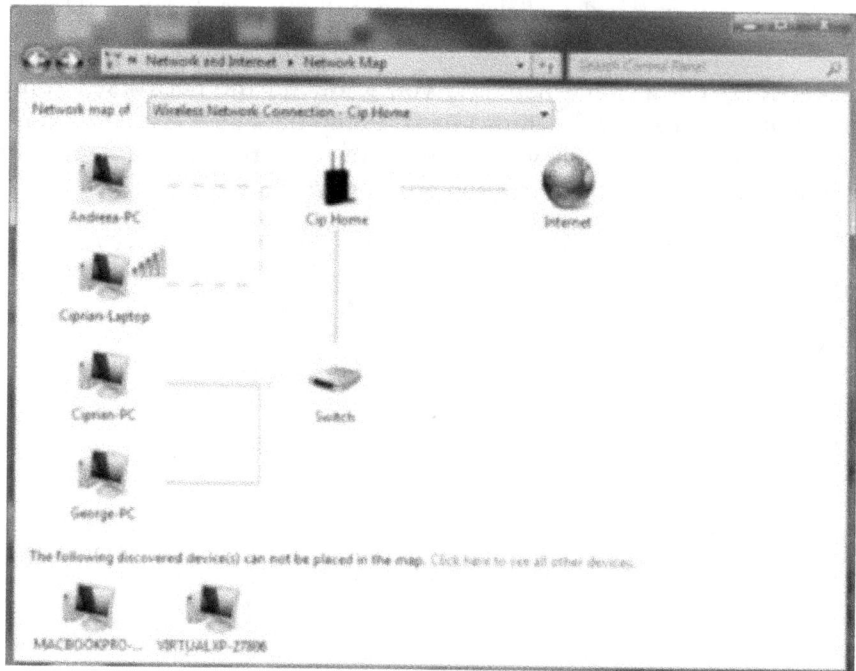
Testing your network

If you don't see icons for the other networked computers, run the Network troubleshooter:

- Click Start.
- Type network trouble (in the Search box).
- Click Identify and repair network problems. This runs the Network troubleshooter, which tries to diagnose the problem.
- Follow the onscreen instructions to diagnose and correct the problem. You can also check the status of your network at any time, from any of the computers on the network. Click Start, Control Panel; then below Network and Internet, click View network status and tasks. Near the top of the window, Windows displays a graphic showing your computer connected to the network, which is connected to the Internet (assuming you set up an Internet connection).

Creating a Homegroup

You can set up a homegroup in Windows, and each user can choose which folders and files to share with other users and networked computers that join the homegroup.

(Only PCs running Windows 7 Premium or Ultimate can create homegroups, but if a networked PC is running the Basic or Starter edition, it can still join a homegroup.)

To create a homegroup, here's what you do:

- Click Start, Control Panel, Choose homegroup and sharing options (below Network and Internet).

- ☐ Click Create a homegroup.
- ☐ Choose the items you want to share, and click Next.

    For example, you may want to share music and photos but not documents.

    Windows displays a password you can use to connect networked PCs to the new homegroup.

- ☐ Jot down the password for future reference and click **Finish**. (You can always view the password on this PC later by performing Step 1 and then clicking **View**.) Windows returns you to the Change homegroup settings page, where you can change your preferences.
- ☐ Click **Cancel**. All user accounts on this computer are now members of the homegroup and can share files.

After you create a homegroup on a PC, this PC and all of its users belong to that homegroup. Each user can perform Step 1 above to access a screen that enables them to choose which libraries they want to share. For other PCs on the network to share files, folders, and other resources, they must join the homegroup, as explained in the following section.

Joining a Homegroup

After you've created a homegroup, other Windows 7 PCs can join the homegroup by performing the following steps:

- ☐ Click **Start**, **Control Panel**, **Choose homegroup and sharing options** (below Network and Internet).
- ☐ Click the **Join now** button.
- ☐ Follow the onscreen instructions to enter the homegroup password and choose the libraries you want to share.

Joining a homegroup

Sharing Files in a Homegroup

These steps work well for sharing the entire contents of your library folders, but say you want to share only certain files or you create a new folder you'd like to share. In such cases, you can choose specifically what you'd like to share (or not share) and how much control over those items other users will have:

- ☐ Click Start, Computer.
- ☐ Navigate to the folder that contains the item(s) you want to share or prohibit other users from sharing. (See Chapter 8 for details about navigating disks and folders.)
- ☐ Click the file or folder to select it. (To select additional items, hold down the Ctrl key while clicking them.)
- ☐ Click Share with (in the toolbar near the top of the window).
- ☐ Click the desired share option: Nobody (to block access), Homegroup (Read), Homegroup (Read/Write), or Specific people.

☐ If you chose Specific people, use the File Sharing dialog box to select the people to share with and specify the level of access for each person; then click Share and then Done.

Checking an Item's Share Setting

To determine whether a resource is shared, click it and then check the details pane (shown in Figure), which shows whether the item is shared and with whom.

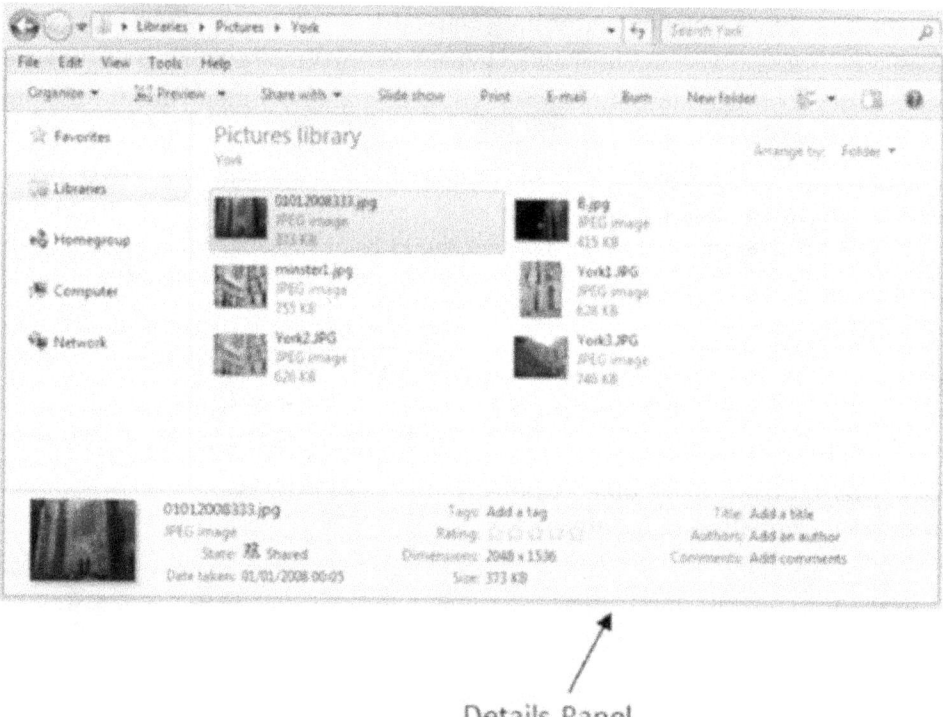

Details Panel

Accessing Shared Disks, Folders, and Files

Your network is up and running and you've chosen to share libraries or folders on the networked computers. Now, how do you get to those shared files and folders? Simply click **Start, Computer**. In the navigation pane (left), below Network, click the desired homegroup or computer. The folder pane (right) displays the shared folders or files in the homegroup or on the computer you selected. You can navigate the folders just as if they were stored on this computer,

Printer

You already know what a printer is, now checkout how to install it on web.

Installing a Printer on Your Network

The steps for installing a printer on your network depend on the printer and how it's connected to the network:

☐ **Network printer**: If your printer is connected to the router or is a wireless printer, you install it as a *network printer*, meaning all networked computers access the printer independently (not through another computer).

- **Shared printer**: If your printer is connected to one of your networked computers—for example, with a USB cable—you can set it up as a *local printer* and then share it. Other computers on the network can then access the printer through this computer.

Installing a Network Printer

To install a network printer, follow these steps:

- Click Start, Devices and Printers.
- Click Add a Printer. The Add Printer dialog box appears.
- Click Add a network, wireless or Bluetooth printer, click Next, and follow the onscreen instructions.

After the network printer is set up, you can use it to print documents just as if the printer were connected to your computer. However, if you did not set up the network printer as your default printer, you must select the printer when you choose to print your document

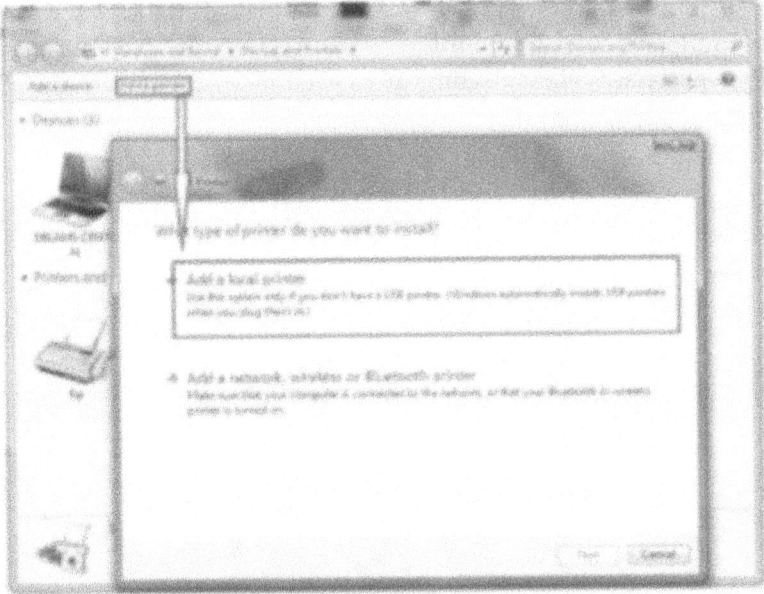

Installing a network printer

Sharing a Printer

To share a printer, first install it as a local printer on one of your networked computers, as explained in earlier . Assuming that the computer that's connected to the printer has joined the network's homegroup, the printer should be available to all computers in that homegroup. If the printer is not available, make sure it's shared:

- Click **Start**, **Devices and Printers**.
- Right-click the printer you want to share and click **Printer properties**.

❏ Click the **Sharing** tab, select the **Share this printer** check box, and click **OK**.

Just like Printer there are other devices also which work like scanner.

Securing Your Network

A broadband Internet connection is typically an *always-on* connection. That is, as long as you leave your modem, router, and computer on, you're connected to the Internet. This makes your network more vulnerable to attacks from snoopy people and perhaps even Internet vandals. With the proper know-how, someone on the Internet can connect to your computer, peek at your documents, and even destroy valuable data. You can't completely protect your computer or network from such threats, but you can significantly deter potential break-ins by implementing various security measures. For details on how to protect your computer and your network from online threats

Points to Remember

- To network your computers, install a single, centralized router and make sure each computer you want on the network has a compatible network adapter or LAN port.
- Learn how to adjust your router settings to enable its firewall, enter encryption settings, and specify a passphrase that all computers need to log on to the network.
- To share files, folders, and other network resources, create a homegroup and have all networked computers join the homegroup.
- To access a shared folder, click Start, Computer, and then click a homegroup or computer (below Network).
- When using your PC in a public Wi-Fi hotspot, change your network location to Public.
- Always have at least one firewall running: the router's firewall when you're home and the Windows firewall when you're on the road

Chapter 2

Disk Operating System (DOS)

As the name suggests, the operating System is used for operating the system or the computer. It is a set of computer programs and also known as DOS (Disk Operating System). The main functions of DOS are to manage disk files, allocate system resources according to the requirement. DOS provides features essential to control hardware devices such as Keyboard, Screen, Disk Devices, Printers, Modems and programs.

Basically, DOS is the medium through which the user and external devices attached to the system communicate with the system. DOS translates the command issued by the user in the format that is understandable by the computer and instruct computer to work accordingly. It also translates the result and any error message in the format for the user to understand.

Brief introduction to DOS and its need

Disk Operating System - is an old operating system prior to Windows that manages everything on your computer: hardware, memory, files...

Many people consider DOS ancient history, with the presence of graphic driven operating systems (GUI - Graphic User Interface) such as Windows, MacOS, I bet no one is running DOS as an operating system. However, the black box becomes useful when you're stuck with Windows, so it's sometimes necessary to know the basics of DOS. Even during the reign of Windows, DOS is still involved in many tasks. Another reason why you should learn DOS is to overwhelm your friends with a bunch of cryptic commands just like in the movies ! DOS isn't that complicated, all you need to know is few commands to list your files, copy, delete, rename, and other stuff...

Getting Started with DOS

Now DOS is known as Command Prompt.

Command Prompt is a feature of Windows that provides an entry point for typing MSDOS (Microsoft Disk Operating System) commands and other computer commands. The most important thing to know is that by typing commands, you can perform tasks on your computer without using the Windows graphical interface. Command Prompt is typically only used by advanced users.

When you're using Command Prompt, the term command prompt also refers to the right angle bracket (>, also known as the greater than character) that indicates the command line interface can accept commands. Other important information, such as the current working directory (or location) where the command will be run, can be included as part of the command prompt. For example, if you open the Command Prompt window and see the C:\> command prompt with a blinking cursor to the right of the right angle bracket character (>), you know that the command you enter will be run on the entire C drive of your computer.

Starting and Working with DOS in Windows 7

Open the Command Prompt window by clicking the Start button, clicking All Programs, clicking Accessories, and then clicking Command Prompt.

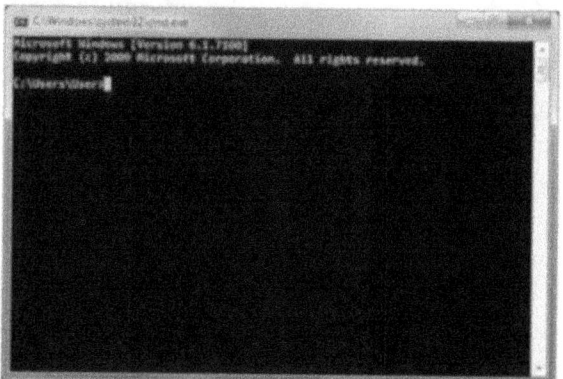

DOS Commands 'cd\,' 'time,' 'date,' and 'cls'

There are set of Command written in DOS for use, some of them, as the name suggests, they are similar to their functions.

Cd: Change Directory - move to a specific Folder

CD (Change Directory) is a command used to switch directories in MS-DOS. For example, if you needed to run Windows 3.11 from DOS, you would type:

cd windows - Changing the directory to Windows;

win - To run the win.com file within the windows directory.

Syntax

Windows XP and later syntax

CHDIR [/D] [drive:][path]

CHDIR [..]

CD [/D] [drive:][path]

CD [..]

.. Specifies that you want to change to the parent directory.

Type CD drive: to display the current directory in the specified drive.

Type CD without parameters to display the current drive and directory.

Use the /D switch to change current drive in addition to changing current directory for a drive.

If Command Extensions are enabled CHDIR changes as follows:

The current directory string is converted to use the same case as the on disk names. So CD C:\TEMP would actually set the current directory to C:\Temp if that is the case on disk.

CHDIR command does not treat spaces as delimiters, so it is possible to CD into a subdirectory name that contains a space without surrounding the name with quotes. For example:

cd \winnt\profiles\username\programs\start menu is the same as:

cd "\winnt\profiles\username\programs\start menu" which is what you would have to type if extensions were disabled.

Windows 98 and earlier syntax

CHDIR [drive:][path]

CHDIR[..]

CD [drive:][path]

CD[..]

Examples

**cd **

Goes to the highest level, the root of the drive.

cd..

Goes back one directory. For example, if you are within the C:\Windows\COMMAND> directory, this would take you to C:\Windows>

Windows 95, 98, and later versions have a feature in the CD command that allows you to go back more than one directory when using the dots. For example, typing: **cd...** with three dots after the cd would take you back two directories.

cd windows

If present, would take you into the Windows directory. Windows can be substituted with any other name.

cd\windows

If present, would first move back to the root of the drive and then go into the Windows directory.

cd\windows\system32

If present, would move into the system32 directory located in the Windows directory. If at any time you need to see what directories are available in the directory you're currently in use the dir command.

cd /d e:\pics

If, for example, you were on the C: drive, typing the above command with the /d option would first switch the E: drive letter and then move into the pics directory.

cd

Typing cd alone will print the working directory. For example, if you're in c:\windows> and you type the cd it will print c:\windows. For those users who are familiar with Unix or Linux this could be thought of as doing the pwd (print working directory) command.

Time: Display or set the system time

Syntax

Displays or sets the system time.

TIME [time]

Type TIME with no parameters to display the current time setting and a prompt for a new one. Press ENTER to keep the same time.

Example

time 12:00

Set the time to 12:00

Date: Display or set the date

Syntax

Displays or sets the date.

DATE [date]

Type DATE without parameters to display the current date setting and a prompt for a new one. Press ENTER to keep the same date.

Example-

date

Display the current date and prompt for a new one. If no date is entered, the current date will be kept.

Cls: Clear the screen

Syntax

CLS

Example-

cls

Running the cls command at the command prompt would clear your screen of all previous text and only return the prompt.

Acquiring Elevated or Administrative Privileges

Some commands that you can run using Command Prompt might require elevated or administrative privileges. To run these commands, you can use the Run as administrator command:

- Click the Start button.
- In the Search box, type command prompt.
- In the list of results, right-click Command Prompt, and then click Run as administrator. If you are prompted for an administrator password or confirmation, type the password or provide confirmation.

Changing Current file type

To convert an existing FAT or FAT32 volume to NTFS, follow these steps:
- Click Start, point to All Programs, point to Accessories, and then click Command Prompt.
- At the command prompt, type the following, where *drive letter* is the drive that you want to convert:
  - convert *drive letter*: /fs:ntfs
  - For example, type the following command to convert drive E to NTFS:
  - convert *e*: /fs:ntfs

Note....

If the operating system is on the drive that you are converting, you will be prompted to schedule the task when you restart the computer because the conversion cannot be completed while the operating system is running. When you are prompted, click YES.

- When you receive the following message at the command prompt, type the volume label of the drive that you are converting, and then press ENTER:
  - The type of the file system is FAT.
  - Enter the current volume label for drive *drive letter*
- When the conversion to NTFS is complete, you receive the following message at the command prompt:
  Conversion complete
- Quit the command prompt.

Creating a File Using the DOS Command 'copy con filename'

Syntax

Copies one or more files to another location.
COPY [/A | /B] source [/A | /B] [+ source [/A | /B] [+ ...]] [destination] [/A | /B]] [/V] [/Y | /-Y]

source	Specifies the file or files to be copied.
/A	Indicates an ASCII text file.
/B	Indicates a binary file.
destination	Specifies the directory or filename for the new file(s).
/V	Verifies that new files are written correctly.
/Y	Suppresses prompting to confirm you want to overwrite an existing destination file.
/-Y	Causes prompting to confirm you want to overwrite an existing destination file.

The switch /Y may be preset in the COPYCMD environment variable. This may be overridden with /-Y on the command line.

To append files, specify a single file for destination, but multiple files for source (using wildcards or file1+file2+file3 format).

Examples

copy *.* a:

Copy all files in the current directory to the floppy disk drive.

copy autoexec.bat c:\windows

Copy the autoexec.bat, usually found at root, and copy it into the windows directory; the autoexec.bat can be substituted for any file(s).

copy win.ini c:\windows /y

Copy the win.ini file in the current directory to the windows directory. Because this file already exists in the windows directory it normally would prompt if you wish to overwrite the file. However, with the /y switch you will not receive any prompt.

copy "computer hope.txt" hope

Copy the file "computer hope.txt" into the hope directory. Whenever dealing with a file or directory with a space, it must be surrounded with quotes. Otherwise you'll get the "The syntax of the command is incorrect." error.

copy myfile1.txt+myfile2.txt

Copy the contents in myfile2.txt and combines it with the contents in myfile1.txt.

copy con test.txt

Finally, a user can create a file using the copy con command as shown above, which creates the test.txt file. Once the above command has been typed in, a user could type in whatever he or she wishes. When you have completed creating the file, you can save and exit the file by pressing CTRL+Z, which would create ^Z, and then press enter. An easier way to view and edit files in MS-DOS would be to use the edit command.

Using the DOS Commands 'type,' 'ren,' and 'del'

- Type: Displays the contents of text files.

    TYPE [drive:][path]filename

    Example-

    type c:\autoexec.bat

    This would allow you to look at the autoexec.bat

- Ren: Used to rename files and directories from the original name to a new name. In earlier releases of MS-DOS instead of using ren or rename you need to use the move command to rename your MS-DOS directories or files.

    Renames a file/directory or files/directories.

    RENAME [drive:][path][directoryname1 | filename1] [directoryname2 | filename2]

    REN [drive:][path][directoryname1 | filename1] [directoryname2 | filename2]

    Note that you cannot specify a new drive or path for your destination.

Examples

rename c:\chope hope

Rename the directory chope to hope.

rename *.txt *.bak

Rename all text files to files with .bak extension.

rename * 1_*

Rename all files to begin with 1_. The asterisk (*) in this example is an example of a wild character; because nothing was placed before or after the first asterisk, this means all files in the current directory will be renamed with a 1_ in front of the file. For example, if there was a file named hope.txt it would be renamed to 1_pe.txt.

rename "computer hope.txt" "example file.txt"

Rename the file "computer hope.txt" to "example file.txt". Whenever dealing with a file or directory with a space, it must be surrounded with quotes. Otherwise you'll get the "The syntax of the command is incorrect." Error

- Del: is a command used to delete files from the computer

    Syntax:

    Deletes one or more files.

    DEL [/P] [/F] [/S] [/Q] [/A[[:]attributes]] names
    ERASE [/P] [/F] [/S] [/Q] [/A[[:]attributes]] names

names	Specifies a list of one or more files or directories. Wildcards may be used to delete multiple files. If a directory is specified, all files within the directory will be deleted.
/P	Prompts for confirmation before deleting each file.
/F	Force deleting of read-only files.
/S	Delete specified files from all subdirectories.
/Q	Quiet mode, do not ask if ok to delete on global wildcard
/A	Selects files to delete based on attributes
attributes	R Read-only files S System files H Hidden files A Files ready for archiving - Prefix meaning not

If Command Extensions are enabled DEL and ERASE change as follows:

The display semantics of the /S switch are reversed in that it shows you only the files that are deleted, not the ones it could not find.

Windows 2000 and Windows XP recovery console syntax

Deletes one file.

del [drive:][path]filename

delete [drive:][path]filename

[drive:][path]filenameSpecifies the file to delete.

Delete only operates within the system directories of the current Windows installation, removable media, the root directory of any hard disk partition, or the local installation sources.

Del and delete do not support replaceable parameters (wild cards).

Examples

Notice: Users who are running Microsoft Windows 95 and are used to deleted items going to the recycle bin need to keep in mind that deleting files from MS-DOS does not send files to the recycle bin.

del test.tmp = Deletes the test.tmp in the directory that you currently are in, if the file exists.

del c:\windows\test.tmp = Delete the c:\windows\test.tmp in the windows directory if it exists.

del c:\windows\temp*.* = (* is for wild character(s)) *.* indicates that you would like to delete all files in the c:\windows\temp directory.

del c:\windows\temp\?est.tmp = (? is a single wild character for one letter) This command would delete any file ending with est.tmp such as pest.tmp or zest.tmp...

Points to Remember

> " **The main functions of DOS are to manage disk files, allocate system resources according to the requirement.**
>
> " **There are set of command written in DOS for use, some of then, as name suggests are similar to their functions.**

Chapter 3

Getting Wired to the Internet

Understanding How Internet Works

The Internet is a worldwide network of computers that can communicate with one another and share resources. The computers are all interconnected by a massive collection of fiber-optic cables, phone lines, and wireless signals that facilitate data transfer at lightning-fast speeds. For your computer to plug into this network and tap its resources, it needs a modem and an Internet service provider (ISP). The modem is the hardware your computer uses to send and receive data on the Internet—it's sort of like a telephone for your computer. The ISP functions as a communications hub between your computer and the Internet. Using the modem, your computer connects to the ISP, and the ISP connects to the Internet.

Picking a Connection Type

Although myriad options are available for connecting to the Internet, they boil down to two choices: dial-up or broadband. Dial-up is a slow connection, but it's available wherever you have access to a phone line, which is pretty much everywhere. Your options may be limited because of your location. Broadband is a fast connection, which you can get through some cable companies, digital satellite services, phone companies, and wireless ISPs, but keep in mind that fast is a relative term. A dedicated (leased) line is typically the fastest, followed by fixed wireless (as opposed to mobile wireless), cable, Digital Subscriber Line (DSL), and satellite, but several factors can affect the actual speed at which your computer connects. One user's DSL connection may be faster than another user's cable connection. If you live in a major metropolitan area, you have plenty of Internet connection types from which to choose: dial-up using a standard modem over your existing phone line, DSL modem, cable modem, satellite, and perhaps even some type of wireless connection (fixed or mobile). Your choice hinges on the following three factors:

- **Availability**: You might not have cable or DSL service in your area, so that can significantly limit your choices. Dial-up service over an existing phone line and satellite service are almost universally available.

- **Speed**: Choose the fastest connection you can afford. You may think you won't use the Internet that much, but when Windows or your other programs need to download huge software updates, you'll be wishing you had a faster connection.

- **Price**: Monthly service charges range from about Rs. 100 per month for dial-up service (plus the cost of local phone service) to more than Rs. 25000 a month for cable or satellite service. (Satellite also costs about Rs. 40000 up front for the installation, although satellite Internet companies often offer special deals if you make a long-term commitment.)

The following sections provide a brief overview of your choices, but you need to shop around to find out what's available in your area and compare prices.

> *Tip...*
>
> Connection speeds are measured in kilobits per second (Kbps), which is equivalent to 1,000 bits per second; and megabits per second (Mbps), which is roughly equivalent to 1 million bits per second.

Turbo-Charging Your Connection with a Cable Modem

Like cable television connections, a cable Internet connection supports high-speed data transfers to your PC, enabling you to cruise the Internet at the same speed you can flip TV channels:

- **Speed**: Rates range from 4Mbps to 20Mbps, although you're likely to experience download rates of 3Mbps to 6Mbps.
- **Cost**: Service depends on speed, plus rent for the modem, which you may get for free or be able to rent from the cable company for a few bucks a month.
- **Drawbacks**: You share bandwidth with other users in your area, so the speed of your connection can fluctuate depending on how many users are currently using the service and how much data they're transferring.

Another Speedy Option: DSL

DSL may be a little more available than cable and cost a little less, but it's also slower:

- **Speed**: Rates range from 768Kbps to 7.1Mbps.
- **Cost**: Service costs depending on the speed, plus for the modem, which you may get for free or be able to rent from the phone company for a few bucks a month.
- **Drawbacks**: Your PC must be within about 3 miles of the phone company's switching station.

Connecting from the Boonies via Satellite

If you can't get cable or DSL, you may need to settle for satellite broadband. Here's how it stacks up:

- **Speed**: Rates range from 500Kbps to 6Mbps but are typically much slower, especially when you're sending data (uploading) from your computer to the Internet.
- **Cost**: Service costs, depending on speed and bandwidth limit, plus Rs. 40000 for the hardware and installation (although the satellite company may waive the installation fee if you make a long-term commitment).

- **Drawbacks**: Satellite service is slower, pricier, and less reliable than cable or DSL service, but it's still way better than dial-up. Also ask whether you have to stick one of those ugly satellite dishes on the side of your house or in your yard.

Tip...

If you choose satellite, consider using a dial-up account as a backup for when you can't connect in storms or dense cloud cover.

On the Go with Wireless Internet

Wireless Internet comes in two basic forms: fixed and mobile. With fixed wireless, you install an antenna on your home or workplace and connect to a specific signal tower. Fixed wireless is beginning to compete with cable, DSL, and satellite, especially in rural areas. Mobile wireless is more like the wireless Internet you might have for an iPhone or similar device. You can connect to the Internet wherever your service provides coverage. Here's how wireless stacks up:

- **Speed**: Speeds vary greatly, typically from 256Kbps to 1Mbps for residential use. With the latest wireless technologies, speeds top out at about 100Mbps for mobile users and 1Gbps for fixed wireless (wireless service for users at stationary locations), but residential users will see speeds more in the range of 1Mbps to 10Mbps.

- **Cost**: Costs vary about as much as speeds and are almost always linked to speed. For example, you may pay Rs.100 per month for a 256Kbps connection and Rs.500 for a 1Mbps connection. I've seen ISPs that charge hundreds of bucks per month for 1Mbps service in areas where the only other broadband option is satellite.

- **Drawbacks**: Distance from the communications tower, any obstacles between the tower and your PC, and other factors can negatively affect the reliability and speed of the connection. Most services limit you to a certain number of megabytes or gigabytes per month and charge you for any number of megabytes over that amount.

When shopping for a WISP (wireless Internet service provider) and a wireless modem (adapter), keep the following standards and terminology in mind:

- **Wi-Fi**: For connecting to a wireless network at home or an Internet hotspot, look for modems that support the 802.11g (up to 54Mbps) or 802.11n (theoretically, up to 600Mbps) standard.

- **WiMAX**: This is like Wi-Fi, but potentially faster and with a much greater range. Through a wireless ISP that supports WiMAX (802.16), you can connect to the Internet whenever you're in the ISP's coverage area.

- **LTE**: Long Term Evolution (LTE) is similar to and in competition with WiMAX.

- **3G**: 3G is short for 3rd Generation wireless communications technology. WiMAX and LTE both support 3G standards.

- **4G**: This high-performance wireless technology supports downloads of up to 1 gigabyte per second (1GBps) for fixed wireless and 100Mbps for mobile users. This is about 10 times faster than with 3G. As of the writing of this book, WiMAX and LTE were evolving toward the

4G standard, and many communications companies were offering the LTE version of 4G. When you're in the market for a WISP, check out the major providers first, including AT&T, Verizon, and Sprint. Visit their websites and enter your phone number or location to determine whether the WISP provides coverage for your location and whatever areas you travel to most.

Chugging Along with Dial-Up

Because dial-up is the least expensive and most universally available of the lot, the dial-up modem has managed to hang on, but dial-up really can't compete when it comes to speed:

- **Speed:** You'll get 56Kbps tops, but you're likely to see speeds in the range of 28Kbps to 44Kbps for downloads and slower for uploads.
- **Cost:** Expect to pay Rs.500 to Rs.1000 per month.
- **Drawbacks:** S-L-O-W.

Dial-up modems are fairly standard, so any new 56Kbps V.92/V.44 modem from any of the major manufacturers (3Com, Zoom, or U.S. Robotics) can handle the job. If you have an open expansion slot in your PC, consider buying an internal modem. If you'd rather use your PC's expansion slots for something else, purchase a USB model.

Most dial-up modems support voice applications, fax, and videophone, but check the product description if you plan to use those features.

Shopping for an Internet Service Provider

The best way to shop for an ISP is to ask your neighbours and/or local business associates which ISP they use and how they like it. This way, you know the service is available in your area and you can find out about any customer service issues the company may have.

The second-best way to shop for an ISP is to connect to the Internet and search the web for services in your area. You can use a friend or relative's computer, or head down to the public library and use one of its computers.

If you have no way to shop for an ISP online, employ one of the following old-fashioned techniques:

- Call your phone company. Most phone companies offer DSL and wireless Internet service—and if they don't, they'll be able to refer you to a company that does. Also, ask about package deals.
- Call your cable or satellite company. If you have cable or satellite TV service, your cable or satellite company probably offers Internet service, too. Ask about package deals, especially if you're already a customer.
- Look in your Yellow Pages under "Internet." Most phone books list the ISPs in the area.

Establishing a Connection

If you're getting a broadband connection through your ISP (such as cable, satellite, or DSL), your ISP is going to schedule a date and time for installation, and the installer will set up your connection for you. You'll have an "always on" connection, in which you remain connected as long as your PC, broadband modem, and router (if you use a router) are turned on. If you choose dial-up service, the ISP provides you with Internet connection settings you must enter to establish a connection, including a phone number, login name, and password. You must then enter the connection settings in Windows:

- Click Start, Control Panel, Network and Internet, Network and Sharing Centre.
- Below Change your network settings, click Set up a new connection or network.
- Click Set up a dial-up connection and click Next.
- Follow the Create a Dial-up Connection wizard's instructions to enter the settings required to establish a connection with your ISP.

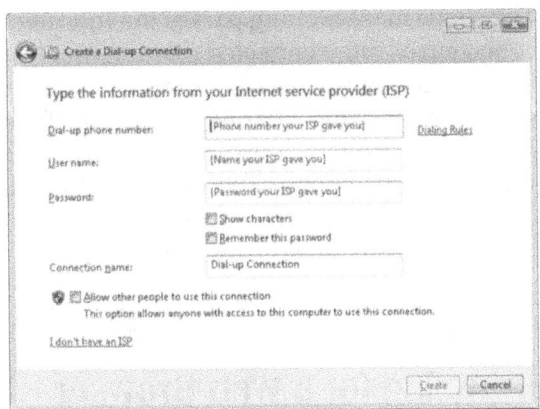

Establishing a dial-up connection

With a dial-up connection, your modem must dial in to the ISP and log on to connect before you can access the Internet. When you install software for most ISPs, the installation places an icon on the desktop that you can click or double-click whenever you want to connect. If you don't see an icon for connecting to the service, here's what you do:

- Click Start, Control Panel, Network and Internet, Network and Sharing Centre.
- Double-click the icon for your dial-up ISP. Windows dials in and automatically enters your username and password to log you in. After you've established a connection, a Dial-Up icon typically appears in the system tray (in the lower-right corner of the Windows desktop). It looks like two overlapping computers. Rest the mouse pointer on the icon to check out your connection speed, or click the icon for additional details. You can right-click the icon and click Disconnect to hang up.

Testing Your Connection Speed

No matter how your computer connects to the Internet, connection speeds can vary depending on the speed of your modem, the condition of the phone and fiber-optic cables, the amount of traffic on the network, and various other factors outside your control. If your Internet connection seems more sluggish than usual, you can check your connection speed at any of several websites:

- Click the Internet Explorer button in the taskbar. The Internet Explorer window appears and then downloads and displays the page it's set up to load upon startup.
- Click in the address bar near the top of the window, type http://us.mcafee.com/root/speedometer/default.asp, and press Enter. This connects you to McAfee's Internet Connection Speedometer.
- Click the Click here to Test Now link. The Internet Speedometer sends data to your computer to test your connection speed and then displays the results.

You can test your actual connection speed on the web.

Poking Around on the World Wide Web

The single most exciting part of the Internet is the World Wide Web (or web, for short), a loose collection of interconnected documents stored on computers all over the world. What makes these documents unique is that each page contains a link to one or more other documents stored on the same computer or on a different computer down the block, across the country, or overseas. You can hop around from document to document, from continent to continent, simply by clicking these links. When I say *documents*, I'm not talking about dusty old scrolls or text-heavy pages torn from books. Web documents contain pictures, sounds, video clips, animations, and even interactive programs.

As you'll see in this chapter, the web has plenty to offer, whatever your interests is¹ – music, movies, sports, finance, science, literature, travel, astrology, body piercing, shopping, you name it.

Browsing for a Web Browser

To navigate the web, you need a special program called a *web browser*, which works through your Internet service provider (ISP) to pull up documents on your screen. Windows 7 includes a web browser called Internet Explorer, but plenty of other (free) browsers are available, including Mozilla Firefox (www.mozilla.com), Google Chrome (www.google.com/chrome), Apple Safari (www.apple.com/safari), and Opera (www.opera.com).

To keep things simple, I use Internet Explorer in the examples throughout this chapter. However, if you're using a different browser, don't fret. Most browsers offer the same basic features and similar navigation tools. Be flexible, and you'll be surfing the web in no time.

Steering Your Browser in the Right Direction

To run Internet Explorer, click its icon (in the taskbar). When your browser starts, it immediately opens a page that's set up as its starting page. You can begin to wander the web simply by clicking links. You can tell when the mouse pointer is over a link because the pointer changes from an arrow into a pointing hand. Click the **Back** button to flip to a previous page, or click the **Forward** button to skip ahead to a page you've visited but backed up from (see Figure). Click on link to flip to a page.

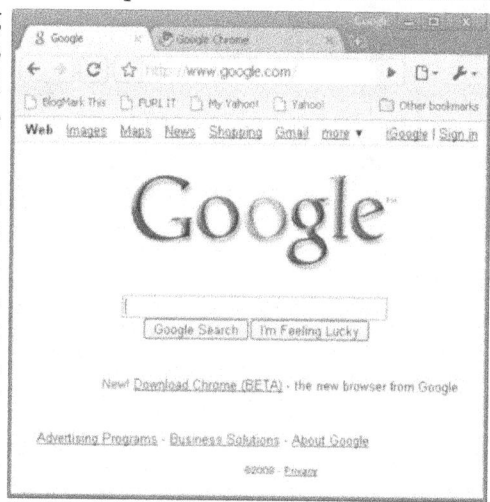

If you click a link and your browser displays a message that it can't find the page or that access has been denied, don't freak out. Just click the **Back** button and try the link again. If that doesn't open the page, try again later. In some cases, the link may have a typo, the page was moved or deleted, or the service hosting the page is temporarily down. On the ever-changing web, this happens quite often. Be patient, be flexible, and don't be alarmed.

A web browser displays and helps you navigate web pages

Note....

If you're not connected to the Internet when you start your browser, it might display a message indicating that it cannot find or load the page. If you have a standard modem connection, reestablish your connection.

A Word about Web Page Addresses

Every website has an address that defines its location, such as www.si.edu for the Smithsonian Institution or www.walmart.com for Walmart. The next time you watch TV or flip through a magazine, listen and keep your eyes peeled for web addresses.

Web addresses are formally called *URLs* (uniform resource locators). URLs allow you to open specific pages. You enter the address in your web browser, usually in a text box near the top of the window, and your web browser loads the page. Every web page URL starts with http://. Newsgroup sites start with news://. FTP sites (where you can get or upload files) start with ftp://. You get the idea. HTTP (short for Hypertext Transfer Protocol) is the coding system used to format web pages. The rest of the address identifies a specific site or page. You can omit the http:// at the beginning, and in almost all cases, you can omit the www. as well. The domain name (site address) is not case sensitive, so joekraynak.com and JoeKraynak.com will both take you to my site, but everything after that might be case sensitive; joekraynak.com/about opens my About page, but joekraynak.com/About results in an error.

Finding Stuff with Google and Other Search Tools

The web has loads of information and billions of pages, and this vast amount of information can make it difficult to track down anything specific. The web often seems like a big library that gave up on the Dewey Decimal System and piled all its books and magazines in the centre of the library. How do you sift through this massive mess of information to find what you need?

The answer: use an Internet search tool. You simply connect to a site that has a search tool, type a couple of words that specify what you're looking for, and click the **Search** button (or its equivalent). The following are the addresses of some popular search sites on the web:

www.google.com   www.yahoo.com

www.ask.com   www.bing.com

Most web browsers have a Search option that connects you to various Internet search tools. Internet Explorer, for example, displays a Search box near the upper-right corner of the window.

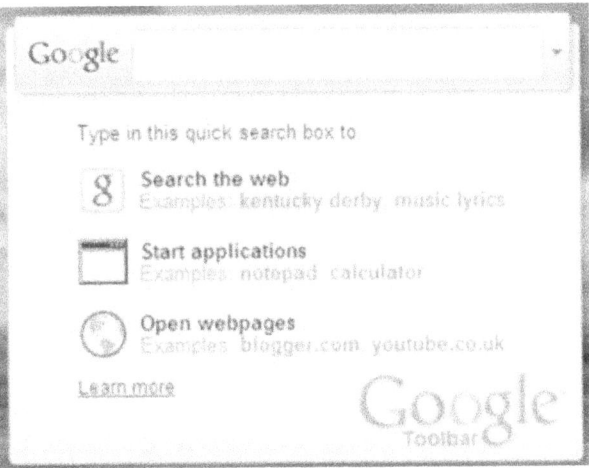

Use the Search box to find the desired web content

Simply click in the Search box, type a couple of key words that describe what you're looking for, and click the **Search** button.

Type your search word or Click phrase in the Search box Search

Locating People Online

You can also use special search tools to find long-lost relatives and friends on the Internet. These search tools are electronic telephone directories that can help you find mailing addresses, phone numbers, and even e-mail addresses. To search for people, check out the following sites:

www.whitepages.com; www.pipl.com

www.spokeo.com; www.anywho.com

www.peekyou.com

The best way to find long-lost friends and relatives, however, is through Facebook.

Navigating Multiple Pages with Tabs

Most web browsers, including Internet Explorer, have tabs that enable you to keep multiple web pages open in a single window. You can then quickly switch to a page by clicking its tab. To open a new tab, click the **New Tab** button, as shown in Figure, or press **Ctrl+T**. By default, Internet Explorer opens a blank tab. You can then click in the address box and enter a website address to open the desired page. If you'd rather have Internet Explorer display the page it opens upon startup rather than displaying a blank tab, take the following steps:

- ❏ Click **Tools, Internet Options**. If you don't see "Tools," click **>>** on the right end of the toolbar.
- ❏ Under Tabs, click the **Settings** button.
- ❏ Click the check box next to **Open only the first home page when Internet Explorer starts** to place a check in the box.
- ❏ To open the home page on new tabs, click the button below "When a new tab is opened, open" and then click **Your first home page**.
- ❏ Click **OK**.

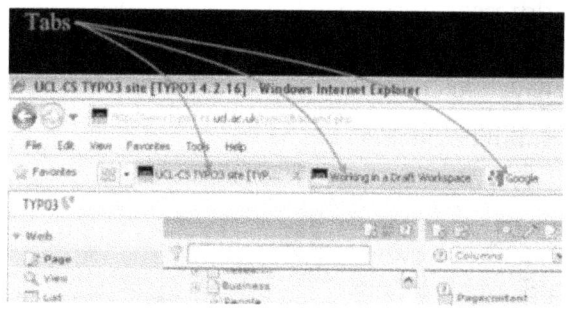

Tabs enable you to open several web pages in a single window

> *Tip...*
>
> *When clicking links, you can choose to have a link's contents open in a new tab or window. Right-click the link and click **Open in New Tab** or **Open in New Window**.*

Going Back in Time with the History List

Although the Back and Forward buttons eventually take you back to where you were, they don't get you there in a hurry or keep track of pages you visited yesterday or last week. For faster return trips and a more comprehensive log of your web journeys, check out the history list.

Click the **Favourites** button (to the left of the tabs) and click **History**. Click the day or week when you visited the website, and click the website's name to see a list of pages you viewed at that site. To open a page, click its name, as shown in Figure.

If you share your computer with someone, you might not want that person to know where you've been on the web. To cover your tracks, do one of the following:

- ❏ Click **Favourites**, **History**; right-click the page, site, day, or week you want to remove; and click **Delete**.

- ❏ Click **Tools**, **Internet Options**, **Delete**. Click to place a check box next to each group of items you want to remove and click **Delete**.

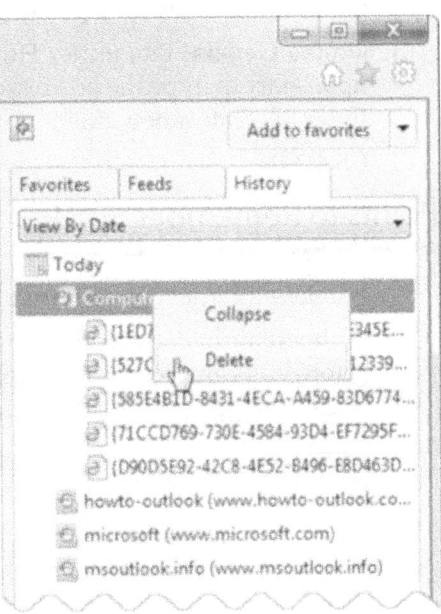

Use the history list to retrace your steps

Marking Your Favourite Web Pages

You can add your favourite sites and pages to the Favourites menu for quick return trips. To mark a page, right-click a blank area of the page and select **Add to Favourites**. You can then add and edit the name of the page as it appears in your favourites list, create a new folder (submenu) to store related favourites, and choose the folder where you want to insert your new favourite. When you're done entering your preferences, click the **Add** button. (Other browsers have similar features but may refer to favourites as *bookmarks*.)

> *Tip...*
>
> *Right-click a blank area of the page and click **Create Shortcut**. This places a shortcut icon for the page on your desktop. To quickly open a favourite page, click **Favourites**, click the folder in which you saved the favourite, and then click the page's name. You can rearrange items on your Favourites menu by dragging and dropping them. If you drag an item over a folder and wait a moment, Internet Explorer opens the folder. You can then drag and drop the item in place.*

Changing the Starting Web Page

Whenever you fire up your browser, it opens with the same page every time. If you have a page you'd like your browser to load upon startup, just let your browser know.

To change your starting page in Internet Explorer, take the following steps:

- Open the page you want to view upon startup.
- Click **Tools, Internet Options**.
- On the **General** tab, under **Home page**, click **Use Current**. To open two or more pages upon startup, type the addresses in the Home page text box, one address per line. (Press **Enter** to create a new line.)
- Click **OK**.

Points to Remember

> " Wireless Internet comes in two basic forms.: fixed and mobile
>
> " With a dial-up connection, your modem must dial in to the ISP and log an to connect before you can access the internet
>
> " Every website has an address that defines its location.

Chapter 4

Google Search, Email and more

Google is a search engine—sort of like a web librarian. It finds stuff on the web, indexes it, and then enables people like you and me to search its index to find what we're looking for, including web pages, photos, video clips, maps, and documents. Performing a basic search on Google is easy and straightforward, but there's much more to it than most people realize.

Performing a Basic Search

To "google" a topic, go to www.google.com, type a brief description of what you're looking for, and click the **Search** button. Google displays links to web pages it deems are most relevant to what you searched for, as shown in Figure. Each item in the search results includes a title, description, address, link to a cached page, and link to similar pages. You can click the title to access the site or page. (A cached page is a backup of a page.) If nothing on the first page of search results looks promising, you can revise your search or scroll to the bottom of the page, where you'll find links to related searches or the next page of search results.

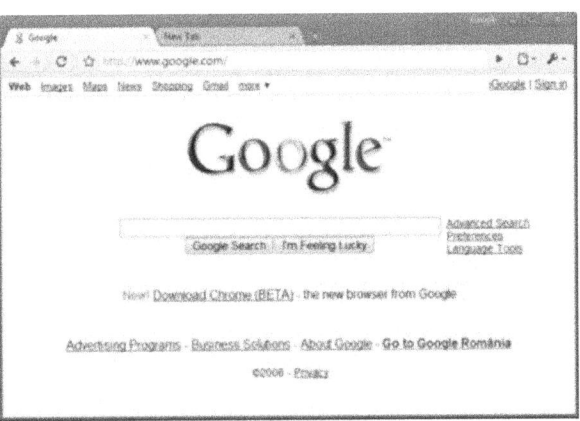

Google a topic of interest

Tip...

If your search phrase contains a typo, Google displays search results for pages that include the typo, along with a link (above the search results) that you can click to perform the search again with the correct spelling. Click the link for more accurate results.

Focusing on Specific Content

You can narrow your search by focusing it on specific content, including images, video clips, blog posts, books, scholarly articles, definitions, and even patents. Before or after performing a search, click one of the content links near the top of the page:

Images, **Videos**, **Maps**, **News**, or **Shopping**. You can click **More** (to the left of the search results) for additional filter options.

Performing an Advanced Search

Unless you specify otherwise, Google uses all the words in your search phrase to present you with what it deems most relevant. You can take more control over the results by performing an advanced search. Go to www.google.com and then click **Advanced Search** (to the right of the Search box). Google's advanced search options appear, as shown in Figure. Enter your search instructions and then click the **Advanced Search** button.

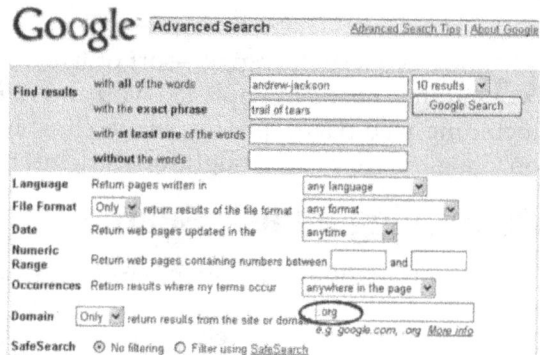

Perform an advanced search

Browsing the Website Directory

Most people search Google for specific information and aren't even aware that they can browse Google by category. If you're not sure what you're looking for, this is a great way to find it. Simply head to directory.google.com and then follow the trail of links to the website or page that interests you.

Adjusting Your Search Settings

Several default settings control the way Google functions and the search results it presents. To check these settings and adjust them, click the **Settings** link in the upper-right corner of any Google page and then click **Search settings**. The Google Preferences page appears, allowing you to enter your preferences for the following options:

- ☐ **Interface Language:** Choose the language you want Google to use when displaying text, tips, and messages.
- ☐ **Search Language:** Choose the language of the pages you want to see in the results.
- ☐ **Safe Search Filtering:** Specify how strict you want Google to be in blocking links to sexually explicit content, including photos and video.

Browse Google's directory

- **Number of Results:** Specify the number of search results you want Google to display per page.
- **Results Window:** You can click the check box to have Google display the search results in a new browser window.
- **Query Suggestions:** You may notice that as you type a search phrase, Google displays a list of search phrases you can choose from so you don't have to keep typing. You can enable or disable this feature.
- **Subscribed Links:** You can subscribe to certain sites to give their content priority in the search results when your search phrase contains specific words. For example, if you subscribe to CalorieLab.com, whenever you include a food item in your search, CalorieLab.com content related to that food item appears at the top of the search results. When you're done entering your preferences, click the **Save Preferences** button.

Cool Google Search Tips and Tricks

Google's Search box can perform all sorts of tricks, including presenting the weather for a specific city, displaying conversion rates for different currencies, converting inches into centimeters, and much more.

To Look Up …	Type (For Example) …
Weather for specific	⇨ city weather Chicago, IL
Stock quote	⇨ ticker BBY
Time in city/country	⇨ time France
News for sports team	⇨ New York Yankees
Calculation result	⇨ (34+27+75)/3
Book author or title	⇨ Ralph Waldo Emerson
Earthquake activity	⇨ earthquake
Temperature conversion	⇨ 65 Fahrenheit in Celsius
Public data	⇨ population WY
People profile	⇨ Sally Strapinski
Definition	⇨ define: quadruped
Local business/restaurant	⇨ pizza Hut
Movie showtimes	⇨ movies Spice
Health issue	⇨ allergy
Poison Control Centre	⇨ poison control
Airline departure/arrival	⇨ Cleartrip
Currency conversion rate	⇨ 300 USD in EUR
Map	⇨ Delhi map
Tracking number for package	⇨ 1X8888Z99999999
Patent number	⇨ patent 4345679
Location based on area code	⇨ 812

Creating a Google Account

Google has numerous features that require you to have a free Google account, including Gmail (web-based e-mail), iGoogle (personal home page), Picasa Web Albums (for photo sharing), Talk (online chat), and Calendar. To tap Google's full potential, I encourage you to create your own Google account:

- ❏ Head to www.google.com.
- ❏ Click **Sign in** (upper-right corner).
- ❏ Below Don't have a Google Account?, click **Create an account now**.
- ❏ Enter the requested information and word verification, review the Terms of Service, and (if you agree to the Terms of Service), click **I accept. Create my account**.

You can now sign in to Google whenever you like, to take advantage of features and tools of Google.

Feature Website Address

Alerts www.google.com/alerts

Free blog www.blogger.com

Bookmarks www.google.com/bookmarks

Calendar www.google.com/calendar

Docs docs.google.com

Gmail mail.google.com

Groups groups.google.com

Customizable home page www.google.com/ig

Maps maps.google.com

Notes www.google.com/notebook

Social network www.orkut.com

Photo sharing picasaweb.google.com

Web aggregator www.google.com/reader

Subscribed links google.com/coop/subscribedlinks

Chat www.google.com/talk

Videos video.google.com

Checking Out Other Search Sites and Tools

Google is the most popular search engine, but it's not the only one. Some of the other search engines are comparable, while others perform specialized searches. Following are some notable search engines you may want to check out:

- ❏ **WhitePages.com** (www.whitepages.com) is excellent for tracking down phone numbers and addresses of individuals and businesses.

- **Yahoo!** (www.yahoo.com) is comparable to Google in connecting you with Yahoo! resources, news, trends, and search.
- **Bing** (www.bing.com) is Microsoft's search engine.
- **Open Directory** (www.dmoz.com) is a hand-crafted, no-frills search directory.

Sending and Receiving E-Mail

How would you like to send a message to a friend and have it arrive in a matter of seconds? Send dozens of messages every day without paying a single cent in postage?

Never again stare out your window waiting for the mail carrier?

Well, your dreams are about to come true. When you have a connection to the Internet and an e-mail program, all these benefits are yours. Here, you learn how to start taking advantage of them.

Before you set sail on your maiden voyage, you have a choice to make: do you want to use an e-mail client installed on your computer, access your e-mail via the web, or both? Using an e-mail program installed on your computer allows you to download all incoming messages to your computer and read them at your leisure—regardless of whether you're connected to the Internet. E-mail programs also provide enhanced tools for managing messages. Web-based e-mail offers the advantage of being able to access your e-mail from any computer. You simply use a web browser installed on any computer to connect to the site, log in, and send and receive your messages.

Using an E-Mail Program

An e-mail program runs on your computer and connects to your Internet mail server to send messages from and receive messages to your PC. You can use any of several programs to access e-mail, including Outlook, Windows Live Mail (download.live.com/wlmail), Eudora (www.eudora.com), and Thunderbird (www.mozilla.com/thunderbird), to name a few. Versions of Windows prior to Windows 7 include an e-mail program—Outlook Express, Windows Messenger, or Windows Mail. Microsoft Office also includes an e-mail program called Outlook. If you're running Windows 7 and don't have Office, go to one of the websites mentioned in the previous paragraph to download and install the e-mail client of your choice.

Setting Up Your Account

The hardest part about using an e-mail program is setting it up to connect to your mail server—an electronic post office that routes your incoming and outgoing messages to their proper destinations. To set up your e-mail program, you need the following information from your ISP:

- **E-mail address:** Your e-mail address contains some version of your name or nickname followed by the @ sign and your e-mail server's domain name—for example, jsmith@iway.com.
- **Password:** You pick the password or have one assigned to you.
- **Outgoing mail (SMTP):** The Simple Mail Transfer Protocol (SMTP) server is the mailbox where you drop your outgoing messages. It's actually your Internet service provider's

computer. The address usually starts with "mail" or "smtp," as in mail.iway.com or smtp.iway.com.

- **Incoming mail (POP3):** The Post Office Protocol (POP) server is like your neighbourhood post office. It receives incoming messages and places them in your personal mailbox. POP server addresses commonly start with pop or mail, as in mail.google.com, but check to make sure. When you have the preceding information, you must enter it into your e-mail program. To enter e-mail settings in Outlook 2010, click **File**, **Add Account**, and then follow the onscreen instructions to enter your name, e-mail address, password, and any other information required to establish a connection with your e-mail provider. Figure shows the first dialog box in the Add New Account wizard in Outlook 2010. Using your e-mail address and password, Outlook can usually obtain the other settings it requires to access your e-mail server. If it can't connect, you may need to start over and click the option to manually configure your server settings (lower-left corner of the dialog box shown in Figure).

Setting uyp an account

Before you can use your e-mail program, you must set up an account.

Addressing an Outgoing Message

The procedure for sending messages over the Internet varies, depending on which e-mail program or online service you're using. In most cases, you first click the button for composing a new message. For example, in Outlook 2010, you click the **Home** tab and then the **New E-mail** button and use the resulting dialog box, as shown in Figure, to address, compose, and send your message.

Note....

Most e-mail programs, including Outlook, feature an e-mail address book or list of contacts. If a contact is in the address book, you simply start typing the person's name or e-mail address in the To box, and the program completes the entry for you. Or, you can click **To** and select the address from the list.

Type the person's e-mail address
- Click to send the message
- Type your message – Type a brief description of the message

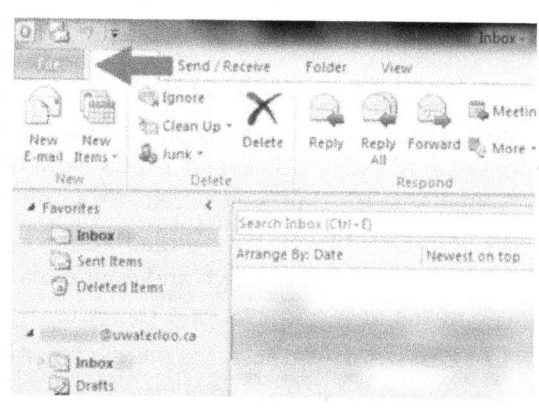

Here's how to send mail with a typical Internet e-mail program (Outlook)

Checking Your E-Mail

Most e-mail programs check for messages automatically on startup or display a button you can click to fetch your mail (the Send/Receive button in Outlook or the Sync button in Windows Live Mail). The program retrieves your mail and then displays a list of message descriptions. To preview a message, click it, as shown in Figure. To view the message in its own window, double-click it. Most e-mail programs use several folders to help you keep your messages organized. For example, Outlook features folders named Inbox, Outbox, Sent Items, and Deleted Items.

To switch from one folder to another, click the desired folder.

Click the message to preview its contents. The contents of the message appear in the preview pane

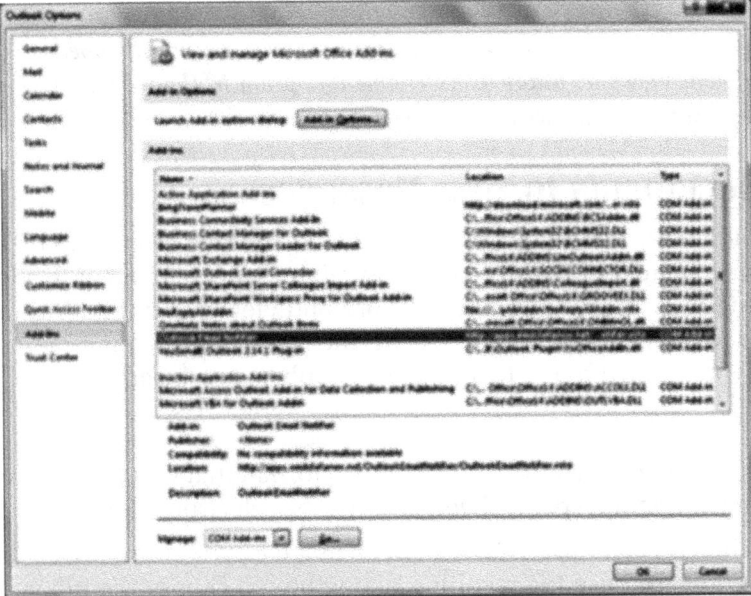

You can quickly display the contents of messages you receive.

Sending Replies

To reply to a message you received, double-click the message, click the **Reply** button, type your reply, and click **Send**. If you received a message that you want to pass along to other recipients, you can *forward* the message. Double-click the message you want to forward, and click the **Forward** button. In the To text box, enter the e-mail addresses of the people to whom you want to forward the message. If you want to add an introduction to or comment about the original message, type this text in the message area. When you're ready to forward the message, click the **Send** button.

Adding Photos and Other Cool Stuff

Almost all e-mail programs, including Outlook, offer a toolbar with buttons for the most common enhancements. You can use the toolbar to make text bold or italic; add bulleted and numbered lists; and insert pictures, horizontal lines, links, and other objects. (If the toolbar does not appear, check the **Format** menu and click the **HTML** or **Rich Text** option. HTML stands for Hypertext Markup Language, the coding system used to format web pages. Rich Text is another specification that allows for fancy formatting in e-mail messages.)

The buttons for inserting pictures and hyperlinks and formatting text work the same way as in your word processing and desktop publishing programs.

To share a link, type the e-mail address or address of the web page you want it to point to and press the **spacebar** or **Enter** key. Most e-mail programs automatically convert web page and e-mail addresses typed in the message area into links. You can also drag links from a web page into the message area and drop them in the message area.

Note....

You have no guarantee that the images and formatting you apply will appear in your message when the recipient views it. Many users enable an option in their e-mail programs to view text only. The e-mail program strips out everything but the text.

Attaching Documents to Your Messages

You can send files along with your messages by creating *attachments*. For instance, if you have a resume you created in Word, you can e-mail it as an attachment to a friend to review. That person could then open the resume in Word and view or print it. Without attachments, you would need to copy the text of the resume and paste it into your e-mail message, losing any formatting you applied to the text and any graphics you inserted.

DEFINITION

An **attachment** is a file in its original condition and format that you clip to an e-mail message. It can be a document, photo, spreadsheet, or any other electronic file.

To send an attachment, compose your e-mail message as you normally do; click the **Attach** or **Insert File** button; and use the resulting dialog box to choose the file you want to send. When you're ready to send the message, along with the attachment, click the **Send** button.

Many word processing and spreadsheet programs have built-in support for e-mail, allowing you to send a document right from the program. In Word 2010, for instance, you can open the document you want to send, open the **File** menu, click **Share**, click **Send Using E-mail**, and click **Send as Attachment**.

If you receive a message that contains an attached file, your e-mail program usually displays some indication that a file is attached. For example, Outlook displays a paperclip icon. If you double-click the message (to display it in its own window), an icon appears at the bottom of the window or in an attachments text box. You can double-click the icon to open the file, or right-click and choose **Save** to save the file to a separate folder on your hard drive.

Note....

When you receive an attachment, use an antivirus program to scan the file before opening it (if it's a document) or running it (if it's a program). Programs are especially notorious for carrying viruses, but documents may contain macro viruses, which can cause as much havoc. (Most antivirus programs are set up to run in the background and automatically scan attachments when you choose to open them or save them to disk.)

What About Free, Web-Based E-Mail?

You've probably heard of "free e-mail" services, such as Gmail (Google Mail), Yahoo!, and Hotmail, and wondered why anyone would need free e-mail. Isn't all e-mail free?

Does your ISP charge extra for it? Of course, your e-mail account is included with the service that your ISP provides; your ISP does not charge extra for it. But there are several good reasons to explore these free e-mail services:

- Free e-mail is typically web-based, allowing you to send messages and check your mail from anywhere in the world using any computer that's connected to the Internet.
- Free e-mail lets everyone in your home or business have his or her own e-mail account.
- Free e-mail is good to use when you register "anonymously" for free stuff, keeping your real e-mail address private.
- Free e-mail also provides you with a stable e-mail address so that when you change ISPs, you don't have to change your e-mail address.

To get a free e-mail account, connect to any of the following sites, click the link for free e-mail, register, and follow the instructions at the site to start using your free e-mail account:

- Gmail – mail.google.com
- Yahoo! – mail.yahoo.com
- Windows Live – signup.live.com
- AOL Mail – mail.AOL.com

Emoticons and E-Mail Shorthand

If you want to look like an e-mail veteran, you can pepper your messages with emoticons (pronounced *ee-mow-tick-ons*). These icons look like facial expressions or act as abbreviations for specific emotions. (You might need to turn your head sideways to see the tiny faces.) You can use these symbols to show your pleasure or displeasure with a particular comment, to take the edge off a comment you think might be misinterpreted, and to express your moods.

Emoticon Meaning

:) or :-) I'm happy, or it's good to see you, or I'm smiling as I'm saying this.

(You can often use this to show you're joking.)

:D or :-D I'm really happy or laughing.

;) or ;-) Winking.

:(or :-(Unhappy. You hurt me, you big brute.

;(or ;-(Crying.

:| or :-| I don't really care. Straight face. Neutral.

:/ or :-/ Skeptical. Annoyed.

:# or :-# My lips are sealed. I can keep a secret.

:> or :-> Devilish grin.

:p or :-p Sticking my tongue out.

<g> Grinning. (Usually takes the edge off whatever you just said.)

<lol> Laughing out loud.

<jk> Just kidding.

In addition to the language of emoticons, Internet chat and e-mail messages are commonly seasoned with a fair share of abbreviations. The following table offers samples of the abbreviations you'll encounter and be expected to know.

Abbreviation Meaning

AFAIK – As far as I know.

AFK – Away from keyboard.

BRB – Be right back.

BTW – By the way.

CUL8R – See you later.

F2F – Face to face (usually in reference to meeting somebody in person).

Abbreviation Meaning

FAQ – Frequently asked questions. (Many sites post a list of often asked questions, along with the answers. They call this list a FAQ.)

FTF – Another version of "face to face."

FYI – For your information.

IDK – I don't know.

IMHO – In my humble opinion.

IMO – In my opinion.

IOW – In other words.

KISS – Keep it simple, stupid.

LOL – Laughing out loud.

NM, NVM – Never mind.

OIC – Oh, I see.

ROTFL – Rolling on the floor laughing.

TTFN – Ta ta for now.

TTYL – Talk to you later.

E-Mail No-No's

To avoid getting yourself into trouble by unintentionally sending an insulting e-mail message, be sure you use the proper protocol for composing e-mail messages.

The most important rule is to NEVER, EVER TYPE IN ALL UPPERCASE CHARACTERS. This is the equivalent of shouting, and people become edgy when they see this text on their screen. Likewise, take it easy on the exclamation points!!! Avoid sending bitter, sarcastic messages (flames) via e-mail. When you disagree with somebody, a personal visit or a phone call is usually more tactful than a long e-mail message that painfully describes how stupid and inconsiderate the other person is.

Besides, you never know who might see your message; the recipient could decide to forward your message to a few choice recipients as retribution.

Also in a business or educational e-mail, use correct spelling and grammar. Abbreviations for words or sentences, such as CUL8er (for "see you later"), and emoticons may be acceptable in text messaging and e-mailing friends, but they're taboo in formal circles.

If you're in marketing or sales, avoid sending unsolicited ads and other missives. Few people appreciate such advertising. In fact, few people appreciate receiving anything that's unsolicited, cute, "funny," or otherwise inapplicable to their business or personal life. In short, don't forward every little cute or funny e-mail message, "true" story, chain letter, joke, phony virus warning, or free offer you receive. Finally, avoid forwarding warnings about the latest viruses and other threats to human happiness. Most of these warnings are hoaxes, and when you forward a hoax, you're just playing into the hands of the hoaxers. If you think the warning is serious, check the source to verify the information before you forward the warning to everyone in your address book. Virus hoaxes are posted at www.symantec.com/avcentre/hoax.html and vil.nai.com/vil/hoaxes.aspx.

Points to Remember

- To set up a new e-mail account in Outlook, click **File**, **Add Account**, and follow the onscreen instructions.
- To create a new e-mail message, click the **Compose Mail** or **New Message** button or its equivalent in your e-mail program.
- incoming e-mail messages are often stored in the Inbox. Simply click the **Inbox** folder and click the desired message to display its contents.
- To reply to a message, select the message and click the **Reply** button.
- To attach a document to an outgoing message, click the button for attaching a file and select the desired document file.
- DON'T TYPE IN ALL UPPERCASE ... and follow all the other rules of proper e-mail etiquette.

Chapter

You Tube

Forget about ABC, CBS, and NBC. YouTube is way more popular, providing you with free access on demand to an unlimited selection of video clips 24/7. Simply head to www.youtube.com, click a link for a video that looks interesting, and then kick back and watch. Of course, you can do a lot more on YouTube, which is what this chapter is all about.

Searching and Browsing on YouTube

When you go to www.youtube.com, the opening screen displays a sample collection of video clips that members recently added, none of which you may find particularly interesting. If nothing catches your eye, or if you're looking for a specific type of video, you can search for items or browse YouTube's video collection.

Searching for Specific Video Footage

When you know what you're looking for, or at least have a vague notion, click inside the Search box (near the top of the page), type one or more words describing what you're looking for, and then click the Search button. YouTube displays a collection of video clips that match your description, as shown in Figure. Click a clip to play it.

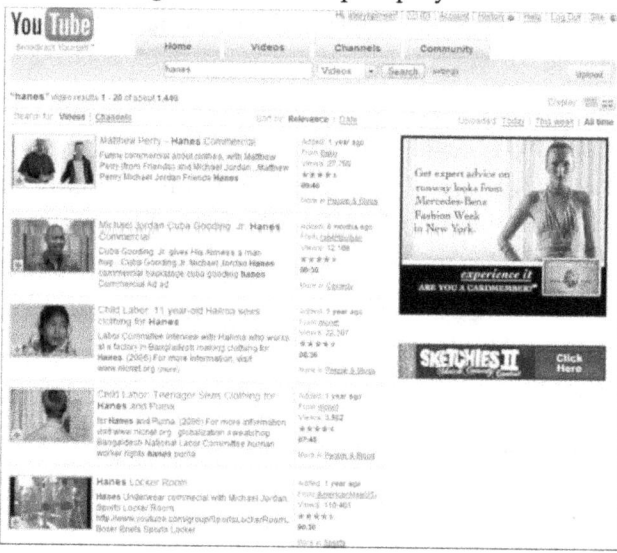

Searching for videos

Browsing YouTube's Video Collection

To browse YouTube's video collection by category, click the Browse button near the top of any YouTube page and then click the double down arrow button to the right of Videos/All categories. Click the category of your choice and then use the resulting screen to browse the videos in the selected category. (See Figure.)

If you click any of the major categories near the bottom of the Categories list, such as Shows or Movies, the Search button changes, so you can limit your search to the selected category. For example, if you click Movies, the Search button changes to Search Movies. Click in the Search box, type one or more words describing the movie, and click Search Movies.

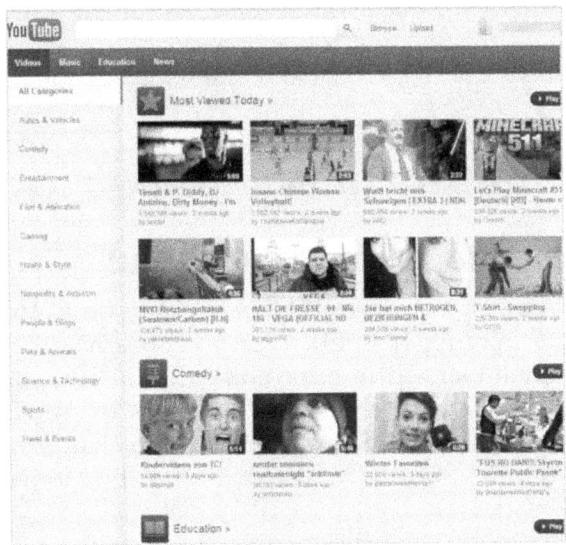

Browse videos by category

Tip...

To return to YouTube's opening page, click the YouTube logo in the upper-left corner of any YouTube page.

Doing more through a YouTube Account

You can watch most videos without joining YouTube, but if you want to do more than that, create an account, which allows you to do the following:

- Enable YouTube to keep track of the videos you watched so it can recommend other videos you might enjoy.
- Flag videos as your favourites, so you can quickly return to them later.
- Rate (thumbs up or down) and comment on videos.
- Subscribe to channels. (A channel is a collection of videos uploaded by a specific individual on YouTube.)
- Customize your YouTube home page.
- Upload and share your own videos with millions of other YouTube users.

Creating an Account

To create an account, click the Create Account link (upper-right corner), complete the form, and click I accept. When YouTube prompts you for your e-mail address, complete the form by entering your e-mail address and the password you want to use (and confirming it), typing the word verification, and then clicking the Create New Account and Finish.

YouTube e-mails you a confirmation message. When you receive it, open the message and click the link to activate your account and verify your e-mail address. This opens YouTube in your web browser and automatically logs you into your account.

Note....

You can sign in to YouTube with your Google account and password.

Signing In and Signing Out

You can sign in to YouTube at any time. Head to www.youtube.com and click the Sign In link (upper right). Type your username and password in the corresponding boxes. To remain signed in after you exit YouTube, make sure the Stay signed in box is checked, or remove the check mark if you want YouTube to sign you out automatically when you leave. Click the Sign in button. If you share your computer with other users, you may want to sign out when you're done watching videos. To sign out, click the Sign Out link (upper right).

Saving Your Favourites

When you come across an amazing video that you're probably going to want to watch again or share with others, add it to your list of favourites. Click the Save to button (below the video) and click Favourites, as shown in Figure.

To view a video on your Favourites list, click your username (upper right) and click Favourites. This displays a list of your favourites. Click the Play button for the favourite you want to watch. (You can remove a video from your list of favourites by clicking the Remove button, to the lower right of the favourite.)

Creating Additional Playlists

Your list of favourites is your default playlist. You can create additional playlists to more effectively organize your favourite videos. To create a playlist, pull up a video you want to add to the playlist, click the Save to button (below the video), and click Create a new playlist, as shown in Figure. Type a name for the new playlist and press Enter. To add a video to your new playlist, pull up the video, click the Save to button, and then click the name of the playlist you want the video added to.

Subscribing to a Channel

If you really like a video, chances are good that you'll enjoy other videos the person has

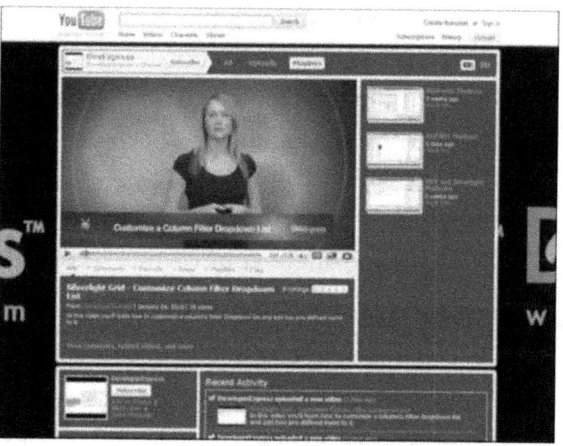

Subscribing to a channel

uploaded. Just above the video, click the member's username to access his or her channel. Here you'll find links to any other videos the member has uploaded, along with the member's favourites and playlists (assuming that the person is not preventing them from being shared). To subscribe to the member's channel, click the Subscribe button at the top of the page or above any video the member has uploaded.

To manage your subscriptions, click the YouTube logo (upper left), click your username (upper right), and click Subscriptions.

Sharing a Video with Others

When you see an incredible (or incredibly funny) video, your first impulse may be to share it with others you think will like it. YouTube provides options that make it easy to share videos via e-mail and on numerous social networking sites, including Facebook and Twitter. To share a video, click the Share button, click the desired share option, and follow the onscreen cues to complete the process.

Sharing a video with others

Rating and Commenting on Videos

Below every video are a thumbs up (Like) button, thumbs down button, and Respond to this video box. Click the thumbs up or thumbs down button to cast your vote for or against the video. To comment on the video, click in the Respond to this video box, type your comment, and press Enter.

If you feel the video is inappropriate, click the Flag button (off to the right), select the reason you think the video is inappropriate, and then click the Flag this video button.

Sharing Your Videos

You may not be Celebrity, but you can play a more active role on YouTube by contributing (uploading) your own video footage taken using a camcorder, digital camera, or even cell phone. You shoot the video, copy it to your computer, edit it, save it as a file, and then upload the file on YouTube. The following sections show you how to deal with the uploading step. If you have a functional webcam attached to your computer, YouTube also enables you to record video on the fly directly into YouTube.

Note....

YouTube has a detailed list of rules and regulations governing the content users can post. Don't post sexually explicit video or video that shows bad stuff, including child or animal abuse, drug abuse, underage drinking or smoking, bomb making, gratuitous violence, racist comments, and so on. I encourage you to read YouTube's Community Guidelines at www.youtube.com/t/community_guidelines before uploading any videos.

Prepping a Video for Uploading

Before uploading a video, edit and save your video to a file that adheres to YouTube's video specifications:

- No longer than 10 minutes
- No larger than 2 gigabytes
- Saved in one of the following file formats:
    - .WMV (Windows Media Video) .3GP (cellphones)
    - .AVI (Windows) .MOV (Mac)
    - .MP4 (iPod/PSP) .MPEG
    - .FLV (Adobe Flash) .MKV (h.264)

Your video editing program, such as Windows MovieMaker or Apple iMovie, enables you to edit and compress video, and should allow you to save the video in one of the acceptable formats. (Keep in mind that compression negatively affects the quality of the video.)

Uploading Your Video to YouTube

After you've prepped your video and have a suitable file to upload, the actual process of uploading it is a snap:

- Click the Upload link (near the top of the page). If the Upload link isn't there, click the YouTube logo in the upper-left corner of any YouTube page to go to your home page, and then click the Upload link.
- Click the Upload video button.

Uploading a video

- ❐ Choose the video file you want to upload, and click Open.
- ❐ Complete the Video information and privacy settings section.

Recording a Video with a Webcam

If you have a functioning webcam connected to your PC, you can use it to record live video and instantly upload it to YouTube. Here's how:

- ❐ Click the Upload link near the top of the page.
- ❐ Click Record from webcam.
- ❐ If an Adobe Flash Player Settings box appears, click Allow to give it access to your webcam, click Remember, so that you won't be asked again, and then click Close. Whatever's in front of the camera should now appear in the record area on the screen.
- ❐ Position yourself or whatever you want to "film" in front of your webcam, click the Record button, and do the recording.
- ❐ If something bad happens while you're recording, click Stop and then Restart.
- ❐ When you're done recording, click the Stop button.

Getting Help

You can do more on YouTube than this chapter covers. To learn about additional features or to obtain assistance using a feature, check out YouTube's help system. Scroll to the bottom of almost any YouTube page and click the Help link. You can then search the help system for a specific topic or browse to learn more about YouTube.

Points to Remember

> - " To search for videos on YouTube, click in the Search box (top of the page), type one or more words to describe what you want, and then click the Search button.
> - " To browse YouTube's video collection, click the Browse link (to the right of the Search button).
> - " Register for a free account so that you can save your favourite videos for future viewing and personalize YouTube.
> - " To save a video as a favourite, click the Save to button (below the video) and click Favourites.
> - " To upload a video of your own, click the Upload link (at the top of almost every YouTube page) and follow the onscreen cues to complete the process.
> - " To get help, scroll to the bottom of almost any YouTube page and click the Help link.

Chapter 6

Twitter

In the twenty-first century, hearing it through the grapevine usually means reading it on Twitter. Twitter is a social networking tool that enables users to share very brief text messages (140 characters or less), commonly referred to as *tweets*. At any time of the day or night, hundreds of millions of Twitter users are in the process of sharing tweets with one another, creating a global buzz. This chapter shows you how to join in the chorus of tweeters round the world.

Creating a Twitter Account

To create a Twitter account, head to twitter.com and click the **Sign Up** button. Complete the Join the Conversation form, shown in Figure. If you don't want to receive e-mail updates from Twitter, click the check box next to **I want the inside scoop** to remove the check mark. Click the **Create my account** button.

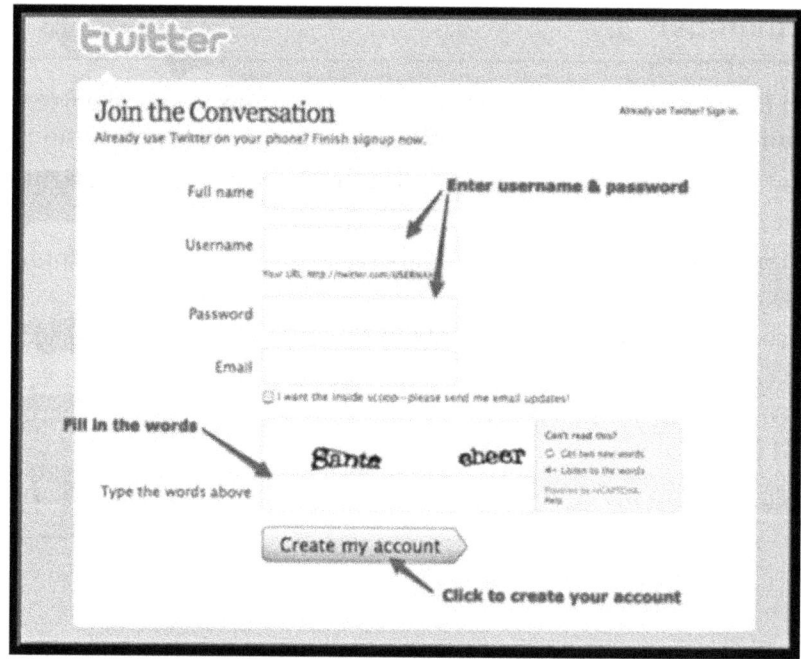

When Twitter asks "Are you human?" click in the **Type the words above** box, type the validation text displayed on the page, and click **Finish**. Twitter creates your account, signs you in, and displays a list of topics you can explore. Before you do that, however, confirm your account. Check your e-mail for a confirmation message from Twitter. When you receive the message, open it and then click the link for confirming your account. Twitter grants you full access to the service and displays its home page.

Signing In and Signing Out

To sign in to Twitter, go to twitter.com, click the **Sign in** button (upper right), enter your username or e-mail address and password in the designated text boxes, and click the **Sign in** button.

When you're done on Twitter, consider signing out, especially if you're sharing the PC—you don't want just anyone tweeting using your username and identity. To sign out, click the **Sign out** link (upper-right corner).

Fleshing Out Your Profile

Unless you add more information about yourself, the only thing identifying you on Twitter is your Twitter name. To give yourself more of a presence and improve your chances of connecting with more people, consider fleshing out your profile with a picture, location, website address, and bio. Click **Settings** (upper right), **Profile**, and use the Profile Settings screen, as shown in Figure, to upload a profile picture and add details about yourself. When you're done, click the **Save** button.

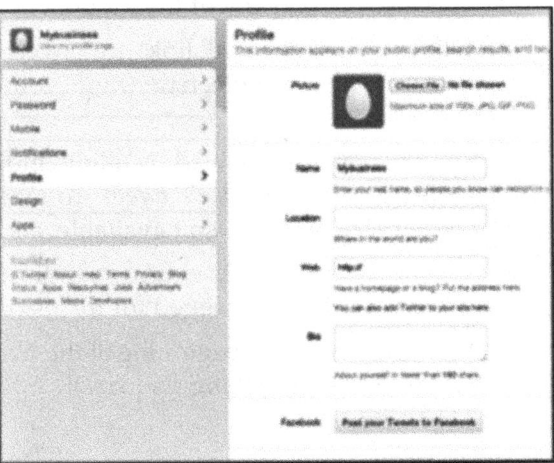

Add a picture and details to your profile.

Tweaking Your Account Settings

Before you post any of your own tweets, you may want to check out your account settings and perhaps make some adjustments. Click **Settings** (upper right) and then **Account**. You can use the Account Settings screen to change your username, e-mail address, language preference, time zone, location, and tweet privacy preference. You can also choose to let others find you by searching for your e-mail address. Enter your preferences and click the **Save** button.

Reading and Replying to Tweets

To get a feel for the Twitter community and tweeting, read some tweets and perhaps reply to a tweet or two before posting your own tweets. The following sections show you how.

Reading a Tweet

When you're interested in learning what others think about a particular topic, you can read all about it on Twitter. On twitter.com, click in the search box, type one or more words describing the topic, and then click the search button, as shown in Figure.

Twitter displays a list of recent tweets (most recent first) that match the topic description you searched. To see more tweets on this topic, scroll to the bottom of the list and click **more**.

Search for tweets:

Every tweet contains the name of the person who posted it, followed by a brief message. You can click the member's name to view more tweets by that individual. Below each message is an indication of the time that has passed since the message was posted. A tweet may also contain any of the following:

Searching for twitter

- ❏ A link (or abbreviated link) to a web page or blog post the person wants you to check out.
- ❏ An "at" sign (@) followed by a link, indicating that the tweet you're reading is actually a reply to someone else's tweet. To read the original tweet, click **in reply to [person's Twitter ID]**, or if this isn't available, click the link to the right of the @ sign.
- ❏ A link preceded by a hashtag (#), indicating a group or extra information. Click the link to view other tweets tagged for inclusion in this group.
- ❏ A retweet icon at the beginning of the tweet (just to the right of the person' profile picture with two arrows making a square).

Tip...

*If you're probably going to search for this same topic in the future, click **Save this search** (above the list of tweets that match your search phrase). Saved searches appear in the navigation bar on the right—simply click the link for the saved search whenever you want to repeat it.*

Replying to a Tweet and Retweeting

Twitter is all about interacting with others—engaging in conversations. If a tweet inspires you to respond in some way, mouse over the tweet and click **Reply**, as shown in Figure. The What's happening? box becomes the Reply to so-and-so box, and Twitter starts you off by adding the @ sign followed by the member's username. Type your reply and then click the **Tweet** button.

Another way to respond to a message is to retweet it—spread the word by passing the tweet along to all

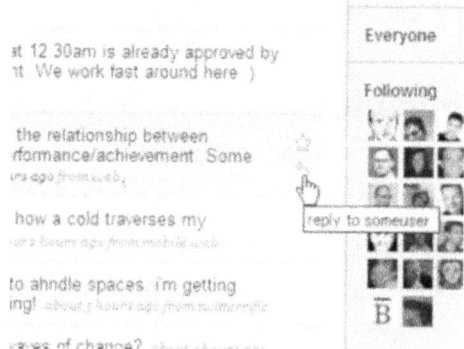

Reply or retweet

of your followers. Of course, when you're just starting out, you probably have few (if any) followers, so retweeting may not make much sense right now. When you do have some followers, here's how you retweet: put the mouse over the tweet you want to retweet, click **Retweet**, and then click **Yes** to confirm.

You can always delete a reply or undo a retweet. To delete a reply you posted, put the mouse over the reply and click **Delete**. To undo a retweet, put the mouse over the tweet you retweeted and click **Undo**.

Flagging a Tweet as a Favourite

When you come across a tweet you'll probably want to return later, mark it as a favourite. Simply put the mouse over the tweet and click the hollow star that appears to the upper right of it. The star turns solid gold, and Twitter adds the tweet to your list of favourites. To view your favourites, click **Favourites** (in the navigation bar on the right).

Posting Tweets

Posting a tweet is a snap. Click in the **What's happening?** box and type a message (140 characters or less). As you type, Twitter displays the number of characters remaining, as shown in Figure—a negative number means you're over the limit.

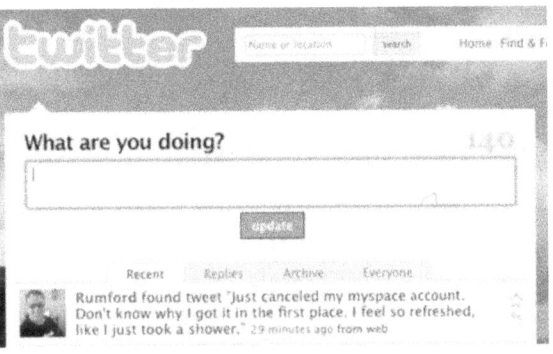

When you're done typing, click the **Tweet** button. Twitter posts your tweet and displays it on your home page.

Your Twitter home page

Adding a Link

Many tweets consist of a brief message that introduces a web page or blog entry followed by a link to that page or entry. To insert a link into your tweet, type the web page address or copy the address from your browser's address box and paste it in your message. (You do not need to include the http:// at the beginning of the address.) When you click the **Tweet** button, Twitter automatically converts the address into a link prior to posting your tweet, so anyone reading it can simply click the link.

Note....

A long URL can consume a huge portion of your allotted 140 characters. Consider using a free URL abbreviation service, such as bit.ly, to truncate the URL for you. Visit bit.ly for details.

Deleting a Tweet

You can't edit a tweet, so if you make a mistake or want to remove your tweet for any reason later, delete it. Sign in to Twitter and rest the mouse pointer on the tweet you want to delete. In the lower-right corner of the tweet, a trash can icon appears with the Delete link next to it. Click **Delete** and then click **OK** to confirm.

Following Users on Twitter

Twitter users who share common interests can choose to follow one another. Friends often use Twitter sort of like Facebook to keep in touch with one another. You and your friends can choose to follow one another—whenever you post a tweet, all your friends are notified. You can also follow complete strangers or politicians, celebrities, athletes, and anyone else who chooses to tweet in public. To follow someone on Twitter, put the mouse over his or her username and click the **Follow** button, as shown in Figure.

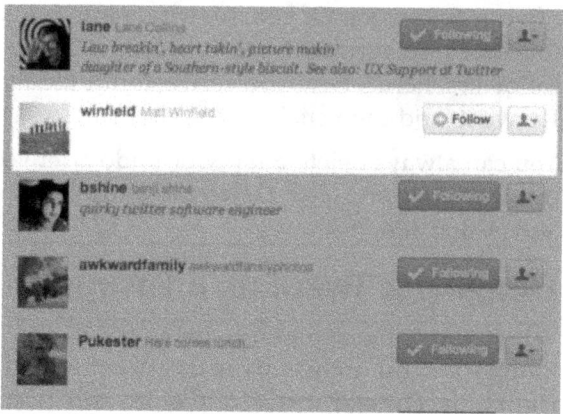

Follow someone on Twitter

Whenever you want to check the person's tweets, click **following** (near the top of the navigation bar).

Searching for People on Twitter

Twitter can help you track down people, businesses, or organizations you may want to follow, assuming they're on Twitter. Click **Find People** (near the top of any Twitter page). In the **Who are you looking for?** box, type the person's or organization's name or e-mail address, and then click **Search**. Scroll down the list, if necessary, to find the individual or organization you're looking for. You can then click the user's name to read tweets or click the **Follow** button to follow that person.

Seeing Who's Following You

If you have friends on Twitter or post such interesting tweets that complete strangers take an interest, you may begin to gather a following. To see who's following you, click **followers** (near the top of the navigation bar). For each follower, Twitter displays the following three buttons:

- ❏ The Follow button enables you to follow the person who's following you.
- ❏ The list button enables you to add users to lists to make them more manageable.
- ❏ The third button opens a menu with options for mentioning so-and-so in a tweet, sending the person a direct message (sort of like e-mail), following the person, blocking the person, or reporting the person for spamming you.

Exchanging Direct Messages in Private

You can send a direct message privately to anyone who's following you. Direct messages are sort of like a cross between an e-mail and a tweet. They're private like e-mail, but brief like tweets. To send a direct message, do one of the following actions:

- ❏ From your home page, click **Direct Messages** (right navigation bar), open the **Send _____ a direct message** list, select the desired recipient, type a message in the box, and click **Send**.

- ☐ Click **followers** (right navigation bar), click the button to the far right of the desired recipient's name, and click **Direct message so-and-so**. Type your message and click **Send**.
- ☐ Click in the **What's happening?** box and type **d+username+message**, dropping the @ symbol; for example, **d bittudon4 What are you working on?** Click the **Tweet** button. As soon as you type **d** followed by a space, the "What's happening?" changes to "Direct message."

*To reply to a follower's tweet with a private message instead of a public response, click **Reply** (below the tweet you want to respond to), replace the @ sign with a d followed by a space, type your message after the person's username, and click **Tweet**.*

Learning More About Twitter

This chapter provides you with all you need to know to start using Twitter, but the more you know, the more you'll get out of it. I encourage you to check out Twitter's help system. Just click **Help** near the top of any page to access Twitter's Help Centre.

Points to Remember

- " To search for tweets about a specific topic, click in the search box (right navigation bar), type a topic description, and click the search button.
- " To post a tweet, click in the **What's happening?** box, type your message (140 characters or less), and click **Tweet**.
- " To reply to a tweet, put the mouse over it, click the **Reply** button, type your reply, and click **Tweet**.
- " To follow someone on Twitter, put the mouse over the person's username and then click the **Follow** button.
- " To personalize Twitter, edit your profile, change your account settings, and more, click **Settings** at the top of most Twitter pages and use the resulting options to enter your preferences

Communicating One-on-One in Real Time

Your PC is no replacement for an iPhone or Android, but when you're sitting in front of a PC equipped with a webcam and microphone, you can do everything you can do with a cellphone and then some ... and for less money. Using programs like AOL Instant Messenger (AIM), Google Talk, and Skype, you can communicate in real time with anyone, anywhere in the world via texting, Internet phone, and even video calling, all for free. This chapter shows you how.

Instant Messaging with AIM

America Online's Instant Messaging program, AIM, is the most popular program of its kind. Millions of people, probably including some of your friends and relatives, use it daily to keep in touch with one another. In the following sections, you learn how to download a free copy of AIM to your PC, install it, and start using it to communicate with your other computer-savvy pals.

Getting Started with AIM

Most IM programs, including AIM, are free for the taking. You don't even need an AIM account. You can use an existing e-mail address, including the address you use to sign in to Facebook. To download and install a copy of AIM and (optionally) create a username that identifies you on the AIM network, take the following steps.

- ❒ Connect to the Internet and start your web browser.
- ❒ Click in the Address bar, type **www.aim.com**, and press **Enter**. AIM's home page appears.
- ❒ Click **Download AIM**.
- ❒ When asked whether to run or save the installation file, click the **Run** button.
- ❒ Follow the onscreen instructions to download and install AIM and set a username and password. (I recommend doing a custom installation so that you can see a list of optional components and choose whether to install them.)

AIM starts automatically after you install it and whenever Windows starts. If you exit the program and decide to restart it later, click **Start**, **All Programs**, **AIM**, and click the icon for running AIM. When AIM starts, it prompts you to enter your username and password.

Type your username and password in the appropriate boxes. To have AIM remember your password so that you don't have to enter it next time, click **Remember me** and **Remember**

my password to place a check in each box. You can also click **Automatically sign me in** and/or **Sign in as invisible** (so your buddies won't know you're online until you want them to). Click the **Sign In** button to go online. At this point, anyone who knows your username can contact you by sending you a message, assuming that you're not invisible.

You can make yourself visible or invisible after signing on. Click the button to the left of your username and choose the desired online status:

- ❏ **Available** lets your buddies know that you're online and taking calls.
- ❏ **Away** lets your buddies know that you're online but away from your PC right now.
- ❏ **Mobile** enables you to set up and turn on IM forwarding so that any instant messages your buddies send you are forwarded to your cellphone.
- ❏ **Invisible** keeps you hidden so that your buddies don't know you're online.

Building a Buddy List

AIM provides a feature called the *buddy list* that enables you to keep track of the people with whom you most commonly interact. To add a buddy to your list, click the **Buddy List** tab, and then click the **+Add** button (just below the tabs) and click **Add Buddy**. The New Buddy window appears. Enter the necessary contact information and your buddy's AIM username and click **Save**. (If you're wondering what an ICQ number is, ICQ is another instant messaging program AIM supports.)

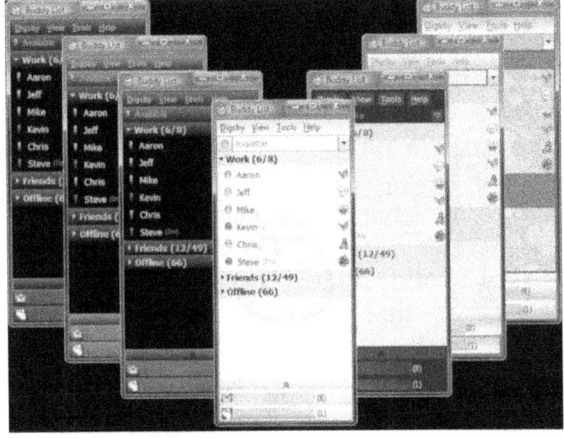

Click the **Buddy List** tab, and then click the **+Add** button (just below the tabs) and click **Add Buddy**. The New Buddy window appears, as shown in Figure.

Add a buddy to your buddy list

Tip...

*If you have loads of buddies, create your own buddy groups to make your buddy list less crowded and overwhelming. To create a new group, click the **+Add** button, click **Add Group**, type a descriptive name for the group, and click **Save**.*

Instant Messaging

Whenever you sign on to AIM, AIM checks to see which of the people on your buddy list are currently online and willing to accept messages. When a buddy is online, you simply double-click that person's username in your buddy list and start chatting.

In addition to typing text, you can format the text to use a different type style, shrink or enlarge the text, add enhancements such as bold and italics, apply highlighting, insert a link to a web page, or even insert small icons that represent your current emotional state. Click the smiley face icon to display a list of available icons for expressing your mood. Click the **A** icon to view formatting tools.

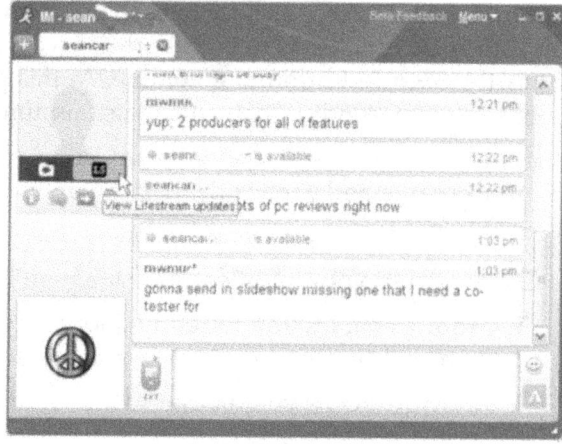

Start sending instant messages!

Audio Instant Messaging

To engage in audio instant messaging with a buddy who has the proper equipment (speakers and a microphone), double-click your buddy's name; then click the camcorder icon and click **Start an Audio IM**. Your buddy then needs to click **Accept** to answer the "phone."

Video Instant Messaging

By equipping your computer with an affordable webcam, you can engage in video calls with colleagues and loved ones. To initiate a video call with AIM, click the camcorder icon and then click **Start a Video IM**. A message pops up on your buddy's screen inviting him or her to a video chat. Assuming that your buddy accepts the invitation, his or her image appears on your screen, as shown in Figure, and your image appears on your buddy's screen.

With video chat, you and your buddy can see and hear one another chat

Texting a Buddy's Mobile Phone

If your AIM buddies have mobile devices with Internet access, you can text them right from AIM, and they can text you back. First, you must enter your buddy's mobile phone number. Right-click your buddy's name and click **Edit Buddy**. Click in the **Mobile Number** box, type the person's 10-digit phone number, and click **Save**.

To text the person, right-click his or her name and click **Text Message (SMS)** or press **Alt+Shift+T**, type your message, and press **Enter**. AIM sends the text message to your buddy's mobile device, and the person can then reply to you.

Getting AIM for Your Cellphone

You can stay in touch with your buddies when you're away from your PC by opening the availability list (to the left of your username) and clicking **Mobile**. When a buddy sends an instant message to your username, the message is automatically forwarded to your cellphone; you can text back a reply, but you can't initiate a discussion.

Sampling Other Chat/Instant Messaging Clients

Although AIM may still be the most popular instant messaging client and chat network around, it's certainly not the only option—and it's not necessarily the best. Following are some other online chat/instant messaging clients you may want to check out, along with website addresses where you can go to learn more about them:

- Yahoo! Messenger, at messenger.yahoo.com
- Google Video Chat and Google Talk, at www.google.com/talk
- Windows Live Messenger, at download.live.com/messenger
- Facebook Chat

If you have a diverse group of friends all using different instant messaging clients, conversing with all of them may mean installing and juggling several different clients. Fortunately, apps that let you access and use multiple services within a single app are available, enabling you to manage and communicate with all your buddies and friends from one account. Following are a few multiprotocol clients you may want to check out:

EBuddy (www.ebuddy.com)

Digsby (www.digsby.com)

KoolIM (www.koolim.com)

Meebo (www.meebo.com)

Miranda (www.miranda-im.org)

Pidgin (www.pidgin.im)

Trillian Astra (www.trillian.im)

Placing Really Cheap (or Free) Phone Calls with Skype

If you're travelling to foreign lands or have friends on the opposite side of the globe, the best way to talk to them is to use Skype or an instant messaging program that supports PC-to-PC and PC-to-phone calling.

For quite a while, the only game in town was Skype, and I think it's still the best, but other players are now competing in this space, including Windows Live Messenger and Yahoo! Messenger. The following sections introduce you to the basics of Skype. Competing services function pretty much the same way.

Note....

If you're wondering what's free and what's not, Skype offers free PC-to-PC calls (audio and video) and instant messaging for Skype users. Skype charges for PC-to-phone calls, and calling a mobile phone costs significantly more. Check www.skype.com for more pricing details and special deals.

Getting Skype

To get Skype on your PC, head to www.skype.com, click **Get Skype**, click **Get Skype for Windows**, and follow the onscreen cues to download and install Skype. (When you click the button to download Skype, a security bar may appear near the top of your browser window. If it does, click the bar to proceed with the download.) When asked whether to run or save the downloaded file, click the **Run** button. When the installation is complete, Skype leads you through the process of creating a new Skype account, creating a Skype username, and entering the e-mail and password you want to use to sign in.

To sign in to Skype, click **Start**, **All Programs**, **Skype**, **Skype**, type your login name and password in the appropriate boxes, and then click **Sign in**. The first time you sign in, a welcome screen appears with buttons you can click to learn the basics, test and set up your equipment (speakers, microphone, and webcam), and find Skype members you may know. If the people you want to call don't have Skype accounts, encourage them to sign up.

Adding Contacts

Skype features several ways to add contacts using a person's Skype username, e-mail address, or phone number:

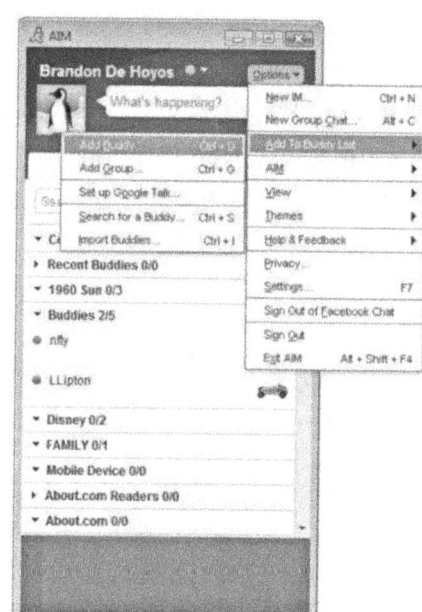

- **Find people using a list of contacts:** Click **Directory** and then click the **See friends who are already on Skype** link. Use the resulting dialog box to find friends on Facebook, AOL, or Gmail, or in your Microsoft Outlook address book, and then add them as contacts.

- **Find someone you know:** Click **Directory**, click in the **Type Skype name** box, type the person's full name or e-mail address, and click **Search**. If the name of the person you're looking for appears in the list near the bottom of the window, double-click it to add it as a contact.

- **Add a phone number:** Click **New**, **New Contact**. Click the **Save a phone number in your contact list** link (near the bottom). Type the contact's name in the **Name** box, as shown in Figure. Open the drop-down list and choose Mobile, Home, Office, or Other. Click the flag and select the country you'll be calling. Click in the phone number box and type the person's phone number. Click **Save phone number**.

Add a contact's phone number

Making Free Skype-to-Skype Calls

You can call, video-call, or instant-message any of your contacts who also use Skype for free, assuming that the person is online, signed on to Skype, and sitting at his or her computer. To place a Skype-to-Skype (PC-to-PC) call, click the person's name in your Contacts list, click the **Skype** tab (if it's not already selected), and then click the Skype places the call, and a notification appears on the screen of the person you called.

Place a Skype-to-Skype call for free

He or she can then answer with or without video or deny the call. Use the buttons near the top or bottom of the call pane to mute your microphone, adjust the volume, turn video on or off, adjust other settings, or hang up, as shown in the figure.

Manage your call session

Cheap Long Distance with PC-to-Phone Calls

Prior to placing PC-to-phone calls, you need to place some money in your account. Click the **View account** button (upper left) or open the **Skype** menu and click **Account**; then use the resulting screen to buy credits or a subscription:

- ❏ **Buy more credit:** For the pay-as-you-go plan, click **Buy more credit** and use the resulting screen and your credit card to add money to your account. As you make calls, money is deducted from your balance.

- ❏ **Buy a subscription:** Click the link to find out more about subscriptions and use the resulting web page to purchase a monthly subscription. This enables you to make unlimited calls for a month for a flat monthly fee at a considerably lower per-minute rate.

- ❏ To place a PC-to-phone call, click the name of the person you want to call in your Contacts list, click the tab for the phone you want to dial, and click the **Call** button, which may appear as Call Phone, Call Home, Call Mobile, or Video Call. When the person answers (or you get the message machine), start talking. When you're done, click the **End call** button (the red button with the phone on it).

Points to Remember

> " Most instant messaging programs allow you to send instant messages to others who use the service and talk with them for free via voice and video.
>
> " To get started with AIM, download the instant messaging client from www.aim.com.
>
> " To add a contact in AIM, click the **+Add** button and then **Add Buddy**, use the resulting dialog box to enter contact information, and click **Save**.
>
> " To contact a buddy who's online, double-click your buddy's name and use the resulting window to exchange text messages or initiate a voice or voice+video call.
>
> " To make free PC-to-PC calls and cheap long-distance calls worldwide, try Skype, at www.skype.com

Chapter 8

Saving and Making Money Online

The World Wide Web is home to one of the largest free-market economies in the world. At any time of the day or night, 7 days a week, 365 (and sometimes 366) days per year, you can find millions of people buying, selling, and giving stuff away online. And because the competition is so stiff among sellers, you can often find better deals online than what local brick-and-mortar discount stores offer. In this chapter, I introduce you to the wonderful world of online shopping and reveal some of the best places to go and strategies to use to find great deals online.

Note....

Don't automatically assume that just because you're buying something online, you're getting a better deal than what local stores are offering. You must still perform your due diligence and compare prices. In addition, buying online usually means you pay shipping fees, which can boost the price of goods higher than what you'd pay locally.

Is It Safe?

Generally speaking, shopping online is about as safe as shopping offline. If you head out to your local shopping mall, for example, you take the risk that someone will break into your car, steal your purse or wallet, or even sneak a peak at the name and number on your credit card. You face similar risks online, but you face these risks whether you shop online or not.

You can reduce the risks by taking the following precautions:

- ❏ Shop only on sites you trust. Buying merchandise from a reputable online retailer is generally much safer than placing an order on an individual seller's website.
- ❏ If you're buying from a little-known company, search the web to find out anything you can about the company. If other shoppers have been burned by that company, they usually post something on the web warning others. enter your name, credit card number, and other sensitive information only on secure websites. You can tell whether a site is secure by looking at the address bar in your browser. The address of a secure site begins with "https" rather than "http." Your web browser may also display a lock icon near the top or bottom of the browser window to indicate that a site is secure.
- ❏ If you receive an e-mail message asking for account information, be highly skeptical. Legitimate companies rarely request account information via e-mail or ask that you log in to a website to verify account information.

- ❑ Don't place orders on a shared computer. Any information you enter on the shared computer could be stored for future use. If it is, someone else can log into the site where you placed the order and access your account information.
- ❑ Pay for orders with a credit card or an escrow service such as PayPal, rather than using a debit card, so you have the opportunity to cancel the order or at least file a dispute if you don't receive your order or are dissatisfied with it. Credit card companies are usually pretty cooperative and successful in ensuring customer satisfaction.
- ❑ Overall, trust your instincts. If a deal sounds too good to be true, it probably is. If a website asks for your UID, birthday, driver's license number, or other information that's rarely needed to process a transaction, it's probably up to no good.

Comparison-Shopping for the Real Deals

Savvy shoppers always compare prices, and you can compare prices online, too. However, several comparison-shopping sites can do all the legwork for you and display a list of merchants who offer the same or similar products.

Myntra is one of many comparison-shopping sites you can find online

Check out the following popular comparison-shopping sites; many also offer product reviews to help you make your decision:

www.flipkart.com

www.naaptol.com

www.myntra.com

Buying Online

The procedure for shopping at most online stores is fairly standard—you find the product you want, check out the product details and what other consumers have to say about it, click a button to order the product or place it in your shopping cart, and check out by entering your payment and shipping information. The Figure pretty much captures the online shopping experience, except for the part when you have to enter your credit card and shipping information. Most dedicated shopping sites make finding and ordering items very intuitive. Select a product category. Go to Myntra.com; Describe the product; Click Go Products that match your product description.

After you've successfully placed your order, the site sends you a confirmation e-mail describing what you ordered, the price of each item, the shipping cost, and your grand total.

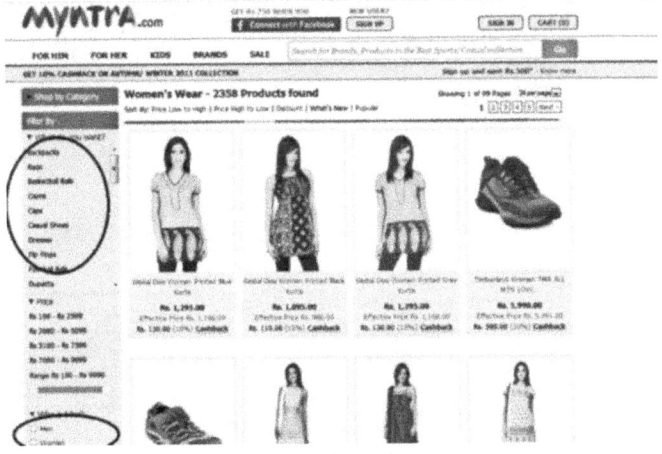

You can search for specific products on Myntra.com

Booking Travel Reservations Online

If you do any travelling, whether for business or pleasure, you can often save considerable amounts of money by serving as your own travel agent and booking your reservations online. Several companies offer one-stop shopping for airline tickets, hotel and motel accommodations, and car rental. Visit the following sites to see what they have to offer:

www.irctc.co.in (Railways)

www.cleartrip.com

www.via.com

Don't stop at simply making reservations online. Plenty of websites offer free information and resources on just about any destination you can imagine. You can go online and check rail routes and schedules and buy your rail pass online.

visit museum websites to plan which exhibits you'd like to see, explore an area's hottest attractions to figure out what you'd like to do, find the best restaurants and entertainment, and much more.

Tip...

Some websites specialize in providing information about your preferred mode of travel. For example, Cleartrip (www.cleartrip.com) can show you how to travel around the world even if you have no travel budget to speak of. If you're looking to trim your travel budget by staying in lower-priced accommodations, via, where you can obtain information about hostels located in just about every country. You can also find sites that specialize in timeshare rentals, cruises, and other special travel opportunities.

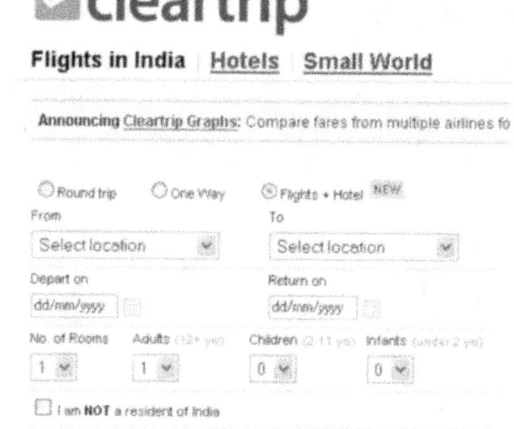

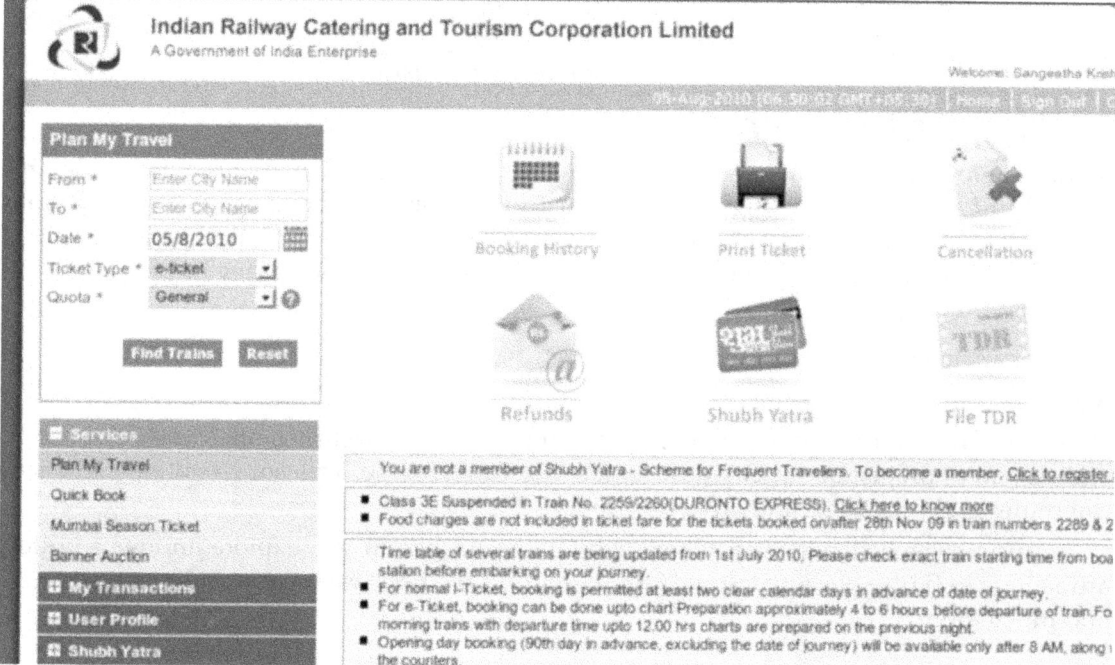

Buying and Selling on eBay

Even if you've never placed a bid or purchased anything on eBay, you've probably heard about it. eBay bills itself as "The World's Marketplace," where its eager community of online sellers and buyers from all around the world gather to buy, sell, and trade products every day. When most people think of eBay, however, they think "online auction," and even though eBay now has its own eBay Stores, it still serves primarily as an online auction.

In the following sections, I step you through the process of buying and selling stuff on eBay, including how you pay for items you buy and collect money for items you sell.

Buying Stuff on eBay

Most people get their first taste of eBay by bidding on and eventually purchasing an item. The process is very similar to buying a product on Amazon.com or from any online store, except that you set the maximum price you're willing to pay for an item. In the following sections, I step you through the process of buying something on eBay. (You can also buy some stuff without bidding if the seller enables the Buy It Now option.)

You don't need to be an eBay member to window-shop on eBay. Point your web browser to www.ebay.in. A Search bar appears at the top of the opening page. Click in the Search box and type one or more words to describe what you're looking for.

To narrow the search to a specific category of products, open the Categories list and click the desired category. Now click the **Search** button. eBay displays a list of items that match your description, as shown in Figure.

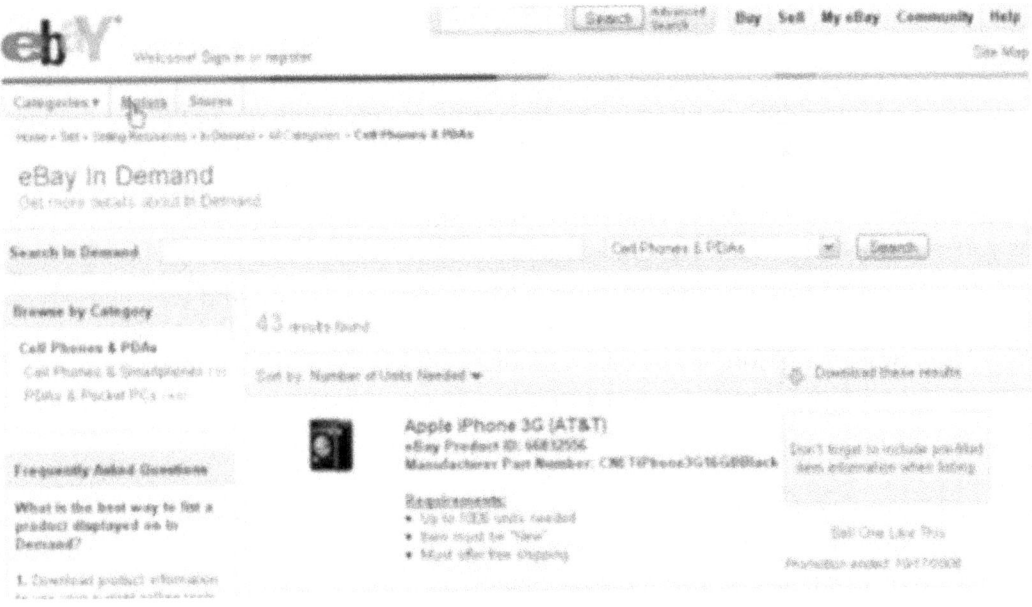

eBay can help you find what you're looking for

Before placing a bid on an item, click the item that interests you to display more information about it. Check the product description to determine whether the item looks and sounds like the product you want.

Also click on the seller's feedback score to view information about the person who has listed the product for sale. eBay encourages buyers to rate sellers and provide feedback so that future buyers know how trustworthy or untrustworthy a particular seller may be. You'll also find a link you can click to ask the seller questions about the product or about payment, shipping, or customer service.

Placing a bid is very easy. Click in the **Your maximum bid** box, type your bid amount, and click the **Place bid** button, as shown in Figure below. (The Your maximum bid box is the minimum amount you can enter to place a bid.

You can learn more about the item and the seller and place a bid

After you place your bid, eBay refreshes the page to show your bid amount as the high bid (or inform you that other eBay users have already bid higher). In a matter of seconds, someone else can enter a higher bid, so if you really want the item, you'll need to keep a careful watch on the bidding activity. You can click the **Watch this item** button to have eBay add the item to a list of items you're interested in. This makes it easier to follow what you're bidding on.

After you win an auction or choose to Buy It Now, eBay sends you and the seller an e-mail message confirming the transaction. Your e-mail message contains a Pay Now button. Click the **Pay Now** button and follow the onscreen instructions to submit your payment.

Tip...

Most eBay sellers accept PayPal payments, so if you plan to make regular purchases, I strongly recommend that you set up a PayPal account at www. paypal.com. PayPal is an escrow service that protects (hides) your primary account information. You fund your PayPal account from your bank or credit card account and use PayPal to buy products, pay vendors, send money to relatives or friends, and so on. The person you pay never sees your bank account or credit card information. PayPal also protects against fraud and insures you against unauthorized payments from your account

After you receive the item(s) you purchase, remember to return to eBay to rate and provide feedback to the seller. Not only do these ratings and feedback help other eBay buyers determine whom they can trust, but positive feedback helps sellers become more successful. Sellers often succeed or fail based on their feedback ratings.

Selling Stuff on eBay

eBay began as a tool to help collectors of Pez dispensers swap dispensers online. From there, it evolved into more of an online flea market, where people would try to sell their collectibles and anything else they no longer wanted to store in their basements or attics. (There's still a lot of that going on.) Now eBay also provides a forum where professional retailers can sell brand-new products.

Note....

Before you list an item for sale, do some research to find out the going price of the item or similar items and see how other sellers are marketing these items online. Using other sellers' marketing materials (photos and product descriptions) is a no-no, but existing product listings can give you some ideas of what works and what doesn't. When you have something for sale, all you have to do is take a photo of it, write a description of it, log on to eBay, and list the item. Keep in mind, however, that eBay charges listing fees, whether or not your item sells. You pay an insertion fee to list an item for sale. This fee varies depending on the type of item and the starting bid or reserve price (the lowest bid you'll accept). The final value fee is calculated as a percentage of the purchase price (rates vary; check eBay's help system, where you can find a link to learn more about seller fees). To sell something on eBay, rest the mouse pointer on **Sell** *(upper-right corner of the page), click* **Sell an Item**, *and follow the onscreen instructions as eBay steps you through the process. eBay assists you in determining how much the item you're selling is probably worth, choosing a category for the item, entering a description, uploading photos, specifying the shipping fee, and so on. After you list an item, you can monitor your auctions to observe the bidding process. When the auction is over, you receive an e-mail message informing you of the winning bid. The buyer then submits the payment, and you package and ship the product.*

Points to Remember

- To shop safely online, stick with well-established stores and place orders only on secure websites, indicated by the closed lock in your browser's notification area, until you gain more experience.
- Comparison-shopping sites such as Flipkart and Naaptol can help you track down the best deals.
- Buying something online usually consists of finding what you want, checking the product details, adding the item to your shopping cart, and checking out.
- On eBay you can buy and sell items through an auction, the Buy It Now option, or an eBay Store.

Chapter 9

Blogs & Web Page

Surfing the web is nice, but you want more. You want to establish a presence on the web, publish your own stories or poems, place pictures of yourself or your family online, show off your creativity, and communicate your ideas to the world.

Where do you start? Right here. This chapter shows you how to whip up your first web page or blog right online, without having to learn any special programs or deal with any cryptic web page formatting codes (unless you really want to). And because you create the page online, you don't have to worry about publishing your web page when you're done.

Behind the Scenes with a Web Page

Behind every web page is a text document that includes codes for formatting the text, inserting pictures and other media files, and displaying links that point to other pages. This system of codes (commonly referred to as *tags*) is called HTML (Hypertext Markup Language). Most codes are paired. The first code in the pair turns on the formatting, and the second code turns it off. For example, to type a heading such as "Apple Dumplin's Home Page," you use the heading codes like this:

1]&36eeaZ 9jbea^c h =dbZ EV\Z1$]&3

The <h1> code tells the web browser to display any text that follows the code as a level-one heading. The </h1> code tells the web browser to turn off the level-one heading format and return to displaying text as normal. Unpaired codes act as commands; for instance, the <img> code inserts a graphic, so <img src='http://www.sample.com/horse.jpg' /> inserts a graphic file named horse.jpg that's stored in the root directory of the website www.sample.com.

Forget About HTML

A basic introduction to HTML is helpful in understanding how the web works, troubleshooting web page formatting problems, and customizing web pages with fancy enhancements, but don't worry—you don't need a certification in HTML to create your first web page. Many companies have developed specialized programs that make the process of creating a web page as easy as designing and printing a greeting card.

Professional web designers use industrial-strength tools like Dreamweaver to design and create websites. If your website needs are modest, however, you can create and format your web pages right on the web simply by specifying your preferences and using forms to enter your text. The next section shows you just how easy it is to create and publish your own web page online with Google Sites.

> *Tip...*
>
> *If you want your own unique domain name with an address like www.yourname.com, a matching e-mail address like bill@yourname.com, and a site with a custom design that's easy to maintain, I recommend starting an account with a web hosting provider—such as Bluehost, HostGator, or GoDaddy.com—and using WordPress to create and maintain your site. (These hosting providers enable you to register a domain name, and they feature numerous tools for creating and maintaining websites and blogs.) It costs around about Rs. 2000 per year to start and maintain, plus Rs. 1500 one-time fee for the Thesis Theme.*

Creating a Free Website with Google Sites

Here's what you do to publish a simple web page (for free) using Google Sites:

- ❒ Using your web browser, go to **sites.google.com**.
- ❒ If you have a Google account, log in. If you don't have a Google account yet, get one: Click **Create an account now** and follow the onscreen cues to enter your desired e-mail address and password.
- ❒ Click the **Create site** button.
- ❒ Click the template you want to use, as shown in Figure. (For more templates, click **Browse the gallery for more**.)

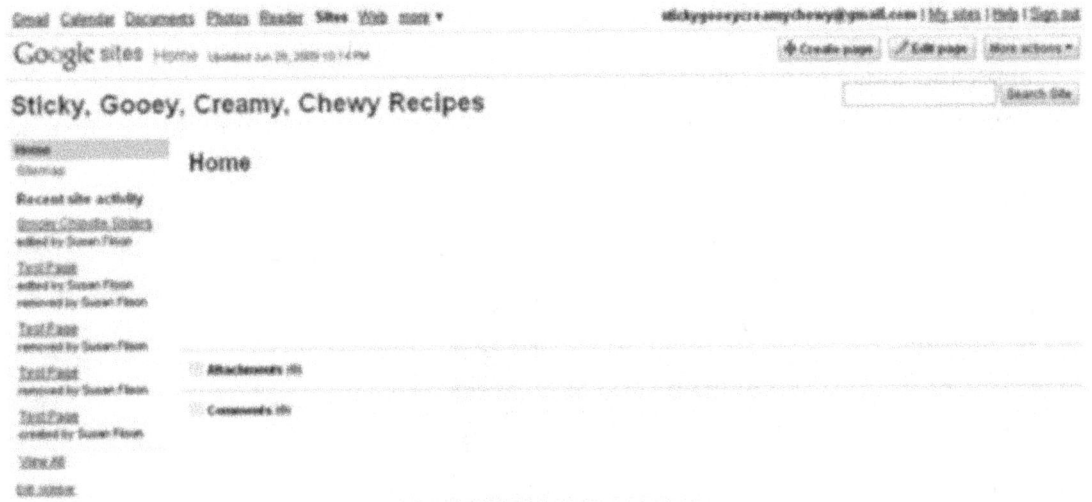

- ☐ Click in the **Name your Site** box and type a name for your site. Google Sites automatically assigns your site a URL (address) based on the name you typed. You can edit the address, if desired.
- ☐ Click **More Options**.
- ☐ Click in the Site description box and type a brief description of your site's content.
- ☐ Under Share with, click **Everyone in the world can view this site** or **Only people I specify can view this site**.
- ☐ If your site contains adult-only content, click **This site contains mature content only suitable for adults**.

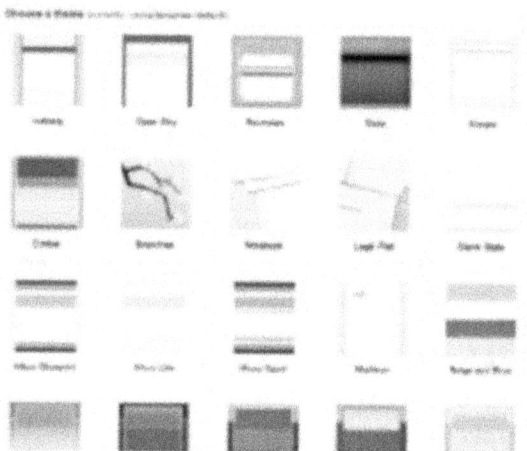

Select a template and enter a name for your site

- ☐ Click in the verification text box and type the verification code that's displayed.
- ☐ Click the **Create site** button. Google Sites creates your website and displays it. The page contains a bunch of placeholder text and graphics you can replace with your own text and graphics. The page also contains links you can click to learn how to replace images, text, and other objects with your own; click one of these links for complete instructions.

Editing Your Google Site

To edit your site, click the **Edit page** button (upper right). The page appears in edit mode, as shown in Figure. To replace text, drag over it and then type your own text. You can use the four buttons in the blue toolbar near the top to do the following:

- ☐ **Insert:** Insert an image, link, table of contents, subpage listing, Google calendar, Google map, and other objects. (See the following two sections for more about inserting objects, apps, and gadgets on a page.)
- ☐ **Format:** Add formatting to create headings; change a paragraph to normal text; add subscripts and superscripts; align text left, right, or centre; and more.
- ☐ **Table:** Insert and manipulate a table by adding or deleting rows and columns.
- ☐ **Layout:** Change the overall page layout—for example, from a three-column layout to a two-column layout, or vice versa.

You can delete or move any of the images or boxed objects on the page. To move an object, hover the mouse pointer over it so that the pointer appears as a four-headed arrow, and then drag and drop the object to the desired location. To delete an object, click it and press the **Delete** key.

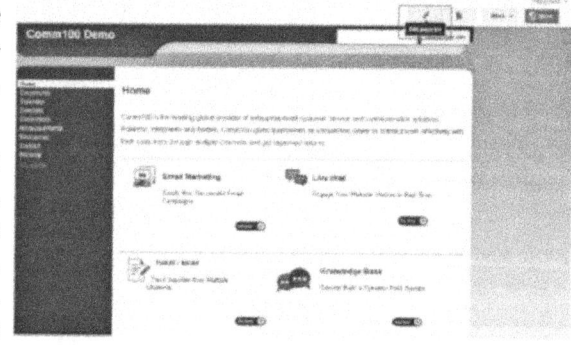

Edit and format text and objects on your site.

The gray toolbar (just above the page) displays buttons for applying standard formatting, such as bold and italic; choosing a type size; creating numbered or bulleted lists; and aligning text left, right, or centre.

Inserting Objects and Apps

Using the Insert menu, you can insert a variety of objects and apps (applications) to make your site more feature rich. Click on the page where you want the object or app inserted, and then follow the instructions for the type of object or app you want to insert (this list includes a small selection of available objects and apps):

- **Image:** Click **Insert, Image** and use the resulting dialog box to upload an image from your PC or use an image from a specific web address. After the image appears in the Add an Image box, click **OK**. Click the image and use the options below it to select an alignment (left, centre, or right), size (small, medium, or large), and word wrap preference (on or off),
- **Video:** Upload the video you want to insert to Google Video or YouTube, and then copy its web address (URL). Click **Insert, Video, Google Video** or **YouTube**. In the resulting dialog box, right-click in the **Paste the URL** box and click **Paste**. Enter any other preferences and click **Save**.
- **Horizontal line:** Click where you want the horizontal line to appear, and then click **Insert, Horizontal Line**.
- **Google Map:** Click **Insert, Map**. In the Search box, type the address of the location you want mapped (including city, state, and zip code) and click **Search**. You can use the controls on the upper left of the map to zoom in or out or pan left, right, up, or down. When the area you want shown appears, click **Select**, enter your preferences in the resulting dialog box, and click **Save**.
- **Picasa Photo:** If you use Picasa to store and manage your digital photos Online, you can easily insert photos from your online photo albums into a Google Sites web page. Click **Insert, Picasa Photo**, use the resulting dialog box to choose the photo to insert, and click **Select**.
- **Picasa Web Slideshow:** If you use Picasa, you can insert an entire photo album to have your Google Site web page display it as a slide show. Copy the web address of the Picasa photo album you want to use. Click **Insert, Picasa Web slideshow**. Right-click the **Paste the URL** box near the top of the resulting dialog box and click **Paste**. Enter your preferences and click **Save**.

Inserting Gadgets

Google includes gadgets you can add to your site to improve navigation and add features to your site. To add a gadget, click where you want the gadget inserted; then click the **Insert** menu, scroll down to near the bottom, and click the desired gadget.

A dialog box pops up requesting additional details. For example, the Recent posts gadget

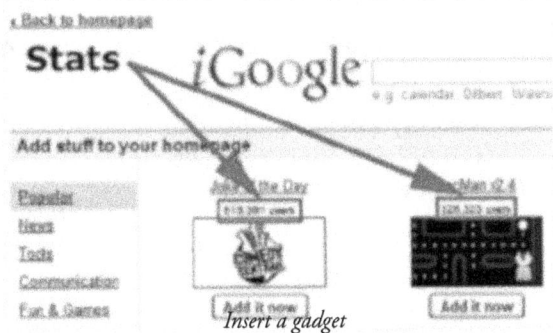
Insert a gadget

displays a list of the most recently published posts, so that visitors can quickly find out what's new on your site. When you choose to add the Recent posts gadget, the dialog box prompts you to specify the type of post, post length, number of posts, and so on.

Saving or Cancelling Your Changes

When you're done making changes to your Google site, you have the option to save the changes or cancel them. To save the changes, click the **Save** button (upper right). To cancel changes, click the **Cancel** button (next to the Save button).

Blogging Your Way to Internet Fame

Relatively recently (sometime in the late 1990s), self-publishing on the web became easier with the introduction of *web logs*, or *blogs* for short. These relatively simple web pages are primarily text based, and you can create and update them by filling out a form. You type a message, comment, or other text and then *post it* to the blog. The most recent posting appears at the top of your blog, followed by prior postings. As your list of posted messages grows, old messages are pushed off the main blog and archived.

The first blogs focused on news and commentary. Bloggers would read an article online and then post a link to the article along with their comments, insights, questions, and sometimes corrections or additional facts concerning the article. Over the years, the scope of blogs has broadened considerably. Now people commonly use blogs to publish their own poetry and fiction; broadcast news stories the mainstream media has overlooked; share business expertise; communicate with family members, friends, and colleagues; promote grassroots movements; keep an online journal; and much more.

Definition

A **blog** (short for **web log**) is a publicly accessible personal journal that enables an individual to voice his or her opinions and insights, keep an online record of experiences, and gather input from others. People also use blogs to share photos with friends and family and set up their own online clubs.

Launching Your Blog

To start blogging, you need a *blogging platform*—an application that provides the tools you need to post messages to your blog and maintain it. Several developers offer platforms for free and can even host your blog for you. The following steps show you how to launch your own blog using the popular WordPress blogging platform:

- Run Internet Explorer and go to **wordpress.com**.
- Click the link to sign up and follow the onscreen instructions to sign up for a WordPress account. When you log in to WordPress, it displays a page that's packed with information and links to other people's blogs.
- Click the **Register a blog** link. If you don't see the link, click the **My Blogs** link (upper-left corner of the page). The Register a Blog page appears.
- Click in the **Blog Domain** box and type a name for your blog. This name will be added to the beginning of wordpress.com to create your blog's domain name. You won't be able

to change this later, although you can delete the blog later and create a new one.

- ☐ Click in the **Blog Title** box and type the title you want to appear at the top of every page of your blog.

- ☐ If you want to prevent search engines from indexing your blog, click the check box next to the Privacy option to remove the check mark.

- ☐ Click the **Create Blog** button. As long as the domain name you entered is not already in use, WordPress displays a message indicating that the domain name is now yours and showing you the username to use to log in.

Register a new WordPress blog for free

You can now visit your blog by entering its address (for example, **yourblogname.wordpress.com**) into Internet Explorer, but it consists of only an opening page that contains a welcome message.

To log in to your blog, launch Internet Explorer, type **yourblogname.wordpress.com/wp-admin** in the address box near the top of the window, and press **Enter**.

You're already logged in, so this displays the WordPress Dashboard for your blog. However, if you log out and then try to use Internet Explorer to go to **yourblogname.wordpress.com/wp-admin** later, WordPress displays a page prompting you to enter your username and password. When you enter the correct information, WordPress displays the Dashboard.

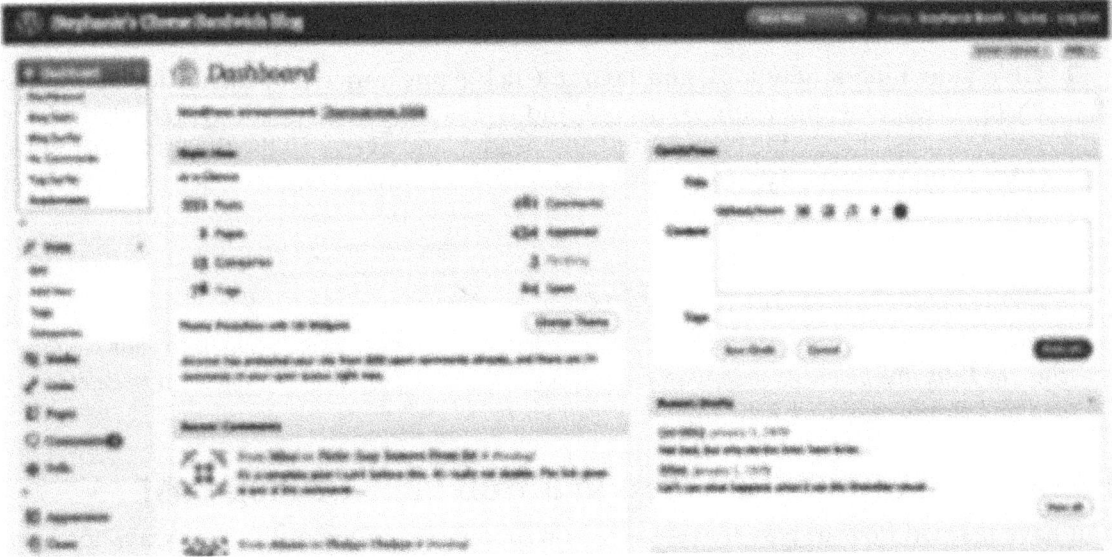

The WordPress Dashboard gives you access to the tools you need to post messages and manage your blog

Making Your Own Blog

The WordPress Dashboard provides all the tools you need to post content to your blog, redesign it, and manage it:

- **Write a new post:** Writing a post is as easy as typing in a word processing application. Click **Posts** (left menu), **Add New**, and then simply type a title for the post, type and format your content, add a photo or other graphic, and click **Publish**. Posts appear on your opening page with the newest post first.

- **Create a page:** Pages are almost identical to posts, but they're used for static content. In other words, they function more like web pages. Links for the pages you create appear under "Pages" in your blog's navigation bar. To create a page, click **Pages** (left menu), **Add New**, and use the resulting form to create your page.

- **Manage your blog:** The Dashboard contains everything you need to manage your blog, and all of it is accessible through the left menu. You can install WordPress upgrades, create and edit posts and pages, create your own media library with digital graphics and video, approve and reject comments others have posted, check your site statistics, and much more.

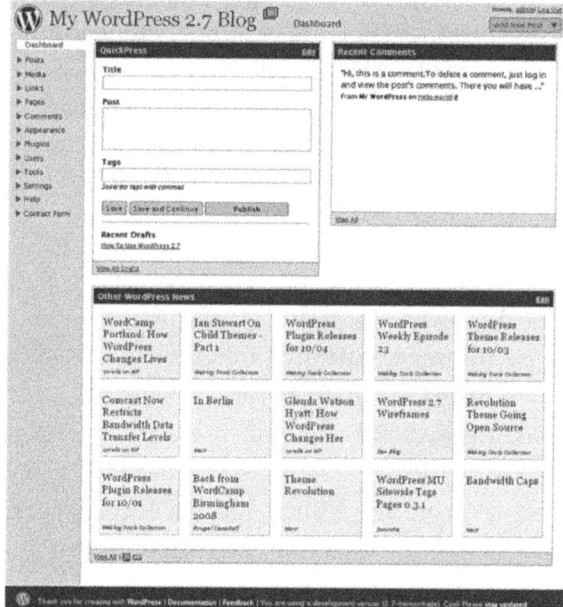

Posting content to your blog is as easy as filling out a form and clicking Publish

- **Give your blog a new look and layout:** Click **Appearance** (left menu) for options to change the theme that controls the look and layout of your blog, add widgets to include new features, change the background and header, and even edit the theme to customize it for your own use. Type a post or page title Formatting buttons Click Publish Enter content here.

𝒩ote....

*If you publish a post or page and regret it later, you can delete or edit it. Log in to your blog, click the **Edit** link below Pages or Posts, scroll down to the end of the entry you want to delete, and click **Remove** or click **Edit** to change your entry.*

Embedding a YouTube Video in a Web Page or Blog Post

You have learned how to watch and share YouTube videos. One of the best ways to share a YouTube video is to include it on a web page or blog. YouTube makes this very easy to accomplish with its *embed* code. The embed code provides a link that pulls the video from

YouTube and plays it on a web page. To embed a video in a web page or blog post, here's what you do:

- ☐ Head to YouTube and display the video you want to embed in your web page or post.
- ☐ Click the **<Embed>** button below the video.
- ☐ Enter your preferences,
- ☐ Click in the box that contains the embed code, and then right-click the code and select **Copy**.
- ☐ Open the post or page you want to add the video to and display it in HTML mode. (This works only if you paste the code into the page's or post's HTML.)
- ☐ Right-click where you want the video inserted and click **Paste**.
- ☐ Save your changes. Now whenever someone opens this page or views this post, they'll see a box in which they can click the play button to view the video. Click to highlight code Enter preferences first.

Points to Remember

> " Hypertext Markup Language (HTML) is a system of codes used to format web pages.
> " You don't need to master HTML to create your own attractive web pages.
> " Google Sites, at sites.google.com, provides an easy (and free) way to build a website.
> " An easy way to establish and maintain a presence on the Internet is to create your own blog.
> " You can place a YouTube video on a web page or blog post by copying and pasting the video's embed code into the HTML for the web page or post.

Chapter 1

Internet Safety

The Internet is a virtual city packed with shopping malls, libraries, community centres, museums, newsstands, meeting rooms, and other valuable offerings. But like any city, the Internet has its dark side—a section of town ruled by vandalism, theft, and other criminal behaviour. You want access to all the positive features the Internet offers, but you need to protect your system, data, and confidential information from the riffraff and from viruses and other *malware*. (Malware is short for "malicious software"—any computer code designed to do something bad.) This chapter shows you how to protect yourself and your PC from various Internet threats.

Keeping Out Viruses and Other Malware

Picking up a virus on the Internet is like coming home from vacation with some exotic illness. You were having so much fun; how could this happen? And how can you prevent it from happening again? By following a few simple rules:

- ❏ Download programs, plug-ins, and add-ons only from reputable and known sites. If you know the company that created the program, go to its web page or FTP server and download the file from there. Most reputable sites regularly scan their systems to detect and eliminate viruses.

- ❏ Don't accept copies of a program from another person (for example, by e-mail). Although the program might not have contained a virus when your buddy downloaded it, your buddy's computer could have a virus that infected the program. Ask your friend where he or she got the file and then download the file from its original location.

- ❏ If your web browser displays a message indicating that a program it's being asked to download is unsigned or from a questionable source, cancel the download.

- ❏ If you receive a file attachment from someone you don't know or from a questionable source, delete the message along with the attachment. Do *not* open it.

- ❏ Keep an antivirus program running at all times. Antivirus programs scan any incoming files for viruses and scan your computer regularly to identify viruses before they can damage files. Two of the best antivirus programs around are also free for home users—Avast (www.avast.com) and Microsoft Security Essentials (www.microsoft.com/

security_essentials/). All you do is download and install them. Either one runs in the background, constantly monitoring activity and incoming files; warns you when they detect anything suspicious; and provides options for dealing with each incident.

Note....

*If you receive e-mail, you'll eventually receive virus warnings indicating that a nasty new virus is infecting thousands of computers all over the world and wiping out hard drives or stealing confidential information. Most of these warnings are hoaxes, and you should not forward the message as it instructs you to do. Check the source of the hoax first. Virus hoaxes are posted at http:// home.mcafee.com/virusinfo (open the **View** drop-down menu below Virus Information and click **Hoax**).*

Detecting and Eliminating Spyware

Spyware is unauthorized software that works in the background to collect information about you or what you type (such as usernames and passwords) and transmits the information to another computer. Fortunately, Windows 7 is equipped with Windows Defender to deal with spyware before it has a chance to do much harm. To access Windows Defender and scan your system for spyware, click **Start** and type **defender** in the **Search programs and files** box. Click **Windows Defender** to run the utility and then click the **Scan** button.

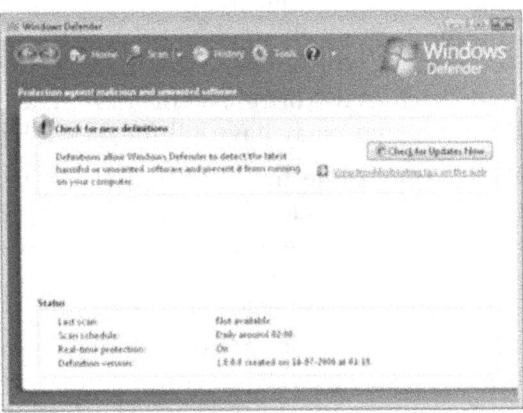

You can scan your PC for spyware

Keeping Hackers at Bay with a Firewall

Whenever you're connected to the Internet, you run the risk of having a mischievous hacker break into your system, steal information, and even damage files. Hackers rarely break into home PCs that are connected to the Internet by a dial-up modem (via a phone line), because you typically disconnect when you're done working. If you have a DSL or cable modem connection, which keeps your computer connected to the Internet at all times, consider installing a *firewall* to prevent unauthorized access to your system.

A firewall stands between your PC and the Internet, enabling your PC free access to the Internet but limiting access to your PC from outside sources (including hackers).

It does this by monitoring activity between your PC or network (*trusted* network) and the Internet (*untrusted* network). As long as the trusted network initiates contact, the firewall allows the connection. If the untrusted network (another PC on the Internet) initiates contact, the firewall blocks the connection.

If you have two or more computers that share an Internet connection through a router, the best option is to use your router's firewall to limit outside access to your networked computers. If your PC is connecting directly to the Internet through a modem or a Wi-Fi connection (not through a router), turn on the Windows Firewall. If your PC works fine with both firewalls on, you have added protection.

Configuring Your Router's Firewall

Your router should have come with instructions that show you how to configure it or at least access the configuration settings. In most cases, you can access the configuration settings by running your web browser and then entering the IP address of your router.

After accessing your router's configuration settings, select the Security or Firewall option and enable the firewall, if it's not already enabled. (It's probably already enabled.)

You can have two or more firewalls in place—your router's firewall (hardware based) and Windows Firewall (software based), for example. If you have an Internet security suite, such as a Norton 360 or McAfee Total Protection, you may have a third firewall.

Running multiple firewalls is fine but may cause problems, such as preventing your PC from accessing the Internet, specific sites, e-mail, or applications on your computer. If you encounter problems, try disabling the software firewalls one at a time until the problem is resolved. See "Activating or Deactivating the Windows Firewall" later in this chapter.

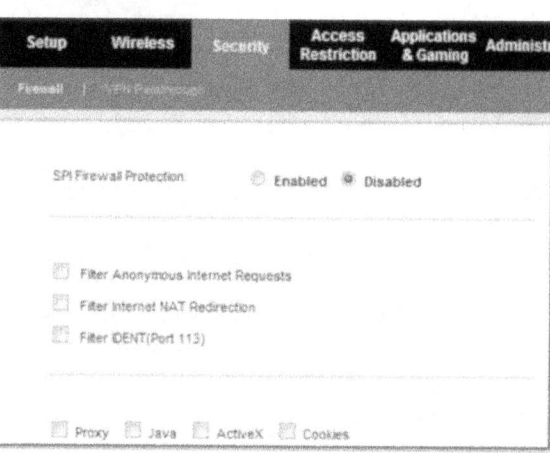

Configure your router's firewall and security settings

Note....

Your PC should always have at least one firewall running when connecting to the Internet—your router's firewall if you're connecting through a router with firewall protection, or Windows Firewall if you're connecting via a Wi-Fi hotspot or other public network.

Limiting Access to Your Wireless Network

Restrict access to your network by enabling encryption and entering a passphrase that all computers on the network must use to establish a network connection.

Check your router's wireless settings to determine whether it has an option to allow the network name to be broadcast. If it does, you can improve security by disabling this option so the router won't broadcast the network name, making your network less visible.

Activating or Deactivating the Windows Firewall

One of the best ways to protect your computer from break-ins is to install a firewall. A firewall is security software that stands between your computer and the Internet, enabling your computer to freely exchange data with the Internet but blocking access to your computer or network from other users on the Internet.

If you're using a router to connect to the Internet, it probably has its own firewall, which is usually superior to any software firewall, such as the Windows firewall.

Activate both your router's and the Windows firewall. (Check your router documentation to determine how to enable/disable its firewall.) If you run into problems connecting to the Internet, try enabling the router's firewall and disabling the Windows firewall. To turn the Windows firewall on or off, follow these steps:

- Click **Start**, **Control Panel**.
- Click **System and Security** and then **Windows Firewall**.
- Click **Turn Windows Firewall on or off**. Enter your log-on password, if prompted to do so, and click **Yes**.
- Below Home or work (private) network location settings, click the desired setting: **Turn on Windows Firewall** or **Turn off Windows Firewall (not recommended)**. Click **OK**.

Note....

Always have at least one firewall running whenever your network is connected to the Internet. For most people, this means all the time.

Making Exceptions for Certain Programs

A firewall can cause Internet connection problems for some features, including instant messaging, especially when you're trying to share files or videoconference. If you experience a connection problem when Windows Firewall is on, you may need to set up exceptions to allow specific programs free access to the Internet.

To set up an exception, click **Start**, **Control Panel**, **System and Security**, **Allow a program through Windows Firewall** (below Windows Firewall). Click the file or program you want to exempt from Windows Firewall protection, and click **OK**.

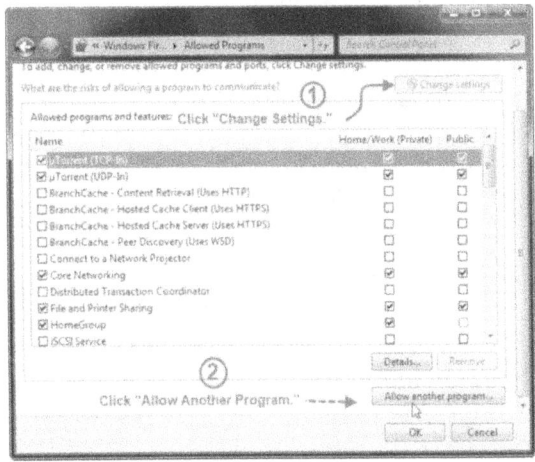

Allow a program to bypass Windows Firewall

Securing Your Portable PC in Public Hot Spots

Wi-Fi is great. You can spend the entire day at Starbucks drinking your caffe latte and playing on your Wi-Fi–enabled laptop. Unfortunately, this makes your PC vulnerable to anyone else in the vicinity who may log on to the Wi-Fi network looking to view or steal information either stored on your computer or passing between your computer and the network. Consider a few tips to protect yourself:

- When you're ready to head out, change your network location to Public: Click **Start, Control Panel, Network and Internet, Network and Sharing Centre**. Below View your active networks, click your current network location and then click **Public network**.
- Be sure you send and receive your e-mail over a secure connection. If you use a web-based e-mail program, you can usually tell whether the connection is secured by looking at the web-based e-mail services address in your web browser. If it starts with "https" instead of "http," you're on a secure site.
- If you use a separate e-mail account, check with your e-mail service provider to determine whether it offers a secure connection. This is usually referred to as SSL (Secure Socket Layer). You'll need to enter special settings in your e-mail program to send and receive e-mail over these secure connections. Your e-mail service provider can give you detailed instructions.
- Don't lug around sensitive data on your notebook computer. None of the other precautions listed here will protect your data if someone walks off with your computer or steals it out of your car. The only protection is to keep sensitive data at home, although this isn't always practical.

Updating Windows 7

Microsoft is constantly improving Windows in all sorts of ways and tweaking it to repair security holes. Assuming that you didn't mess with the Windows update feature, Windows automatically downloads updates when your PC is connected to the Internet and installs those updates either automatically or after receiving your okay.

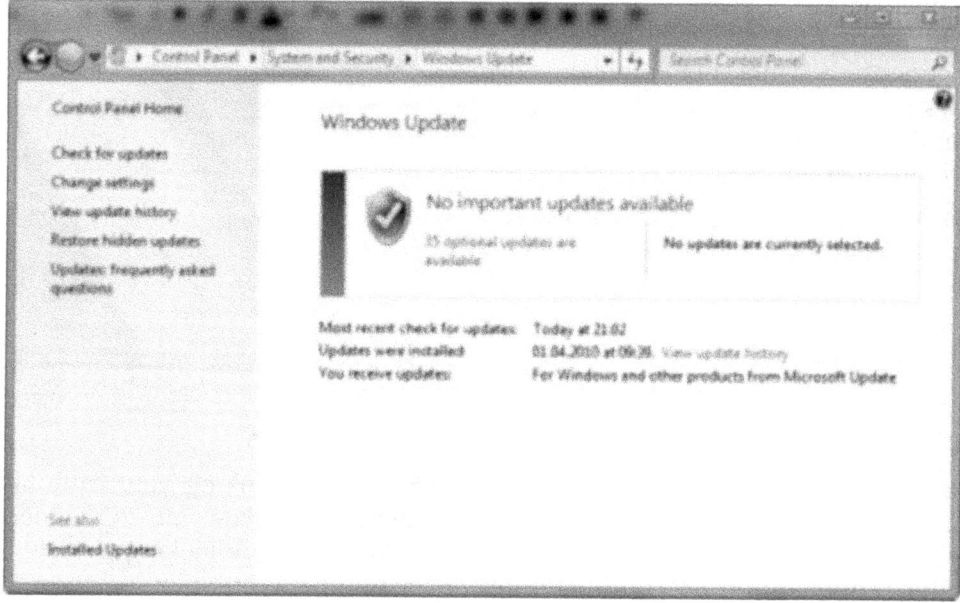

Check for Windows updates

If you disabled automatic updates, be sure to check for and install updates regularly to ensure that you have the latest security updates in place.

To check for updates, click **Start**, **All Programs**, **Windows Update**. Click **Check for updates** (on the left). Windows connects to the Internet, checks for updates, and (if it finds any) displays a link showing the number of updates available, as shown in Figure. Click the link to check out the available updates. You can then choose the updates you want to download and install, and click **OK** to install them. To enable or disable automatic updates and adjust the feature's settings, click **Start**, **Control Panel**, **System and Security**, **Windows Update**, **Change settings**. The Choose how Windows can install updates screen appears, which allows you to enable or disable automatic updates, choose when Windows checks for updates, and adjust other settings.

Opting for a Standard User Account

We have introduced three types of user accounts: Administrator, Standard, and Guest. An administrator account gives you complete control over your PC, but it also poses a security risk. If other users (or hackers) gain access to your PC when any user is logged on as an administrator, they can cause all sorts of trouble.

Consider creating only one password-protected administrator account and using a standard user account for daily PC use. If someone happens to gain access through the standard user account, he won't be able to change settings, create or delete other user accounts, or damage system files. When you're logged on as a standard user, you can still perform administrative tasks, as long as you know the administrator's password.

And if Windows prevents you from performing a specific administrative task, you can switch to your administrator account to proceed with whatever you want to do and then log out when you're done.

Dealing with E-Mail Threats and Annoyances

Many of the most serious threats to your PC come in the form of e-mail or e-mail attachments. By knowing what to watch out for and what to do or not do, you can steer clear of most problems.

Avoiding Infected E-Mail Attachments

The cardinal rule for avoiding viral infections from e-mail attachments is this: never open an e-mail attachment unless you know and trust the source. Your antivirus program will scan incoming e-mail messages and attachments, providing you with some protection, but if the attachment contains a brand-new virus your antivirus program doesn't recognize, or the sender figured out a way to hide the virus's true identity, your antivirus program may not catch it.

Don't Even Preview Junk Mail

You can recognize most junk mail just by looking at the sender's name or the message description, so don't even look at it. Some messages may contain images or other objects that send a message back to the sender, letting the person know that the message arrived and someone looked at it. This tells a spammer that your e-mail address is legitimate.

To avoid looking at junk mail, take the following precautions:

- ☐ Turn off your e-mail client's preview pane. Check your e-mail program's help system for details.
- ☐ Use your e-mail client's junk mail feature to automatically route suspected spam to the junk mail folder. You can then pick through the junk to find legitimate messages and delete the rest.
- ☐ Open e-mail only from known and trusted sources, and immediately delete all the rest.

Avoiding Phishing Scams

Phishing scams are commonly initiated via e-mail. *Phishing* is a fraudulent means of obtaining someone's username and password. The con artist/identity thief sends an e-mail that appears to originate from a bank, credit card company, or other such company warning of a serious issue you must address *right now* by clicking a link and logging into your account. The link takes you to an official-looking site complete with text boxes for entering your username and password. If you enter this sensitive information, the con artist has what he or she needs to log in to your real account.

To avoid falling victim to e-mail phishing scams, take the following precautions:

- ☐ Play it safe and go to the website yourself without clicking the e-mail or a link in the message. (You should be able to identify the website from the subject line or the address from which the e-mail originated.) If the website is legitimate and the message did in fact originate from it, you should be able to find something on the website about it; otherwise, it's most likely a scam.
- ☐ If your e-mail program features phishing protection, enable it. Check your e-mail program's help system for details.
- ☐ Be aware that most legitimate companies do not send alarming e-mail messages with links to click to resolve issues. If you receive such a message, it's probably not from the source it claims to come from.
- ☐ Put the mouse over the link and look in the status bar at the bottom of the window to see the address the link will take you to. Chances are, the link indicates one destination while the address takes you somewhere else entirely. This is a sure sign of a phishing scam.
- ☐ If you think the e-mail message is legitimate, head to the company's website to obtain legitimate contact information, and then contact the company to verify that someone at the company sent the message.
- ☐ If you determine that an e-mail message is fraudulent, report it to the legitimate company from which it supposedly originated so that the company can take action.

Phishing scams are most common but not exclusive to e-mail. Con artists may try to obtain login information in chat rooms, via instant messaging programs, and in social networking venues (including Facebook). A good rule of thumb is this: provide sensitive information only if *you* initiated contact.

Avoiding, Filtering, and Blocking Spam

Spam is unsolicited, unwanted e-mail—junk mail. When you first get an e-mail account, you receive very little spam. The spam starts to flow when you post your e-mail address on the web or sign up for free offers with companies that pass your e-mail address to others. Once your e-mail address lands on a spam list as a legitimate address, the spam is almost impossible to stop. When it comes to spam, an ounce of prevention is worth a kilo of cure. Here are a few tips for preventing spam:

- ❒ Don't use your primary e-mail address to register for anything on or off the web. Get a free e-mail account from Gmail, Yahoo!, or Hotmail and use this disposable e-mail address to register for stuff. If you start receiving too much junk e-mail, you can dump the address and use a different one.
- ❒ If you receive a spam message, don't reply to it. Replying verifies your e-mail address to the spammer and encourages more spam.
- ❒ Don't put your primary e-mail address on the web—for example on your website or blog. Spammers scan the web for e-mail addresses.

If you're receiving an overwhelming amount of spam, try the following solutions to slow the flow:

- ❒ Log in to your Internet service provider's website to find out whether it uses a spam blocker and whether you can configure it to make it more aggressive in identifying spam.
- ❒ If you have the e-mail account through a hosting provider (a business that hosts your website), log in to your account to find out about available options.
- ❒ Purchase and install a spam blocker of your own. You can find plenty of good spam filters/blockers out there, including SPAMfighter (www.spamfighter.com), ChoiceMail (www.digiportal.com), and Spameater Pro (www.spameaterpro.com), to name a few.

Most newer e-mail programs offer some sort of spam protection (perhaps in the form of a Junk Mail folder) and enable you to enter settings to make the program more or less aggressive in identifying spam. In addition, you can usually create lists of safe senders and blocked senders and block e-mail from certain domains or countries. Search your e-mail program's help system for "spam" to determine what, if any, spam protection features are available.

Checking Your Browser's Security Settings

Your web browser has its own security guard on duty that checks incoming files for potential threats. If you try to enter information such as a credit card number on a form that's not secure, the web browser displays a warning message asking if you want to continue. If a site attempts to install a program on your PC, your browser displays a confirmation dialog box or a warning near the top of the window asking for permission to download and install the program.

With most browsers, the default security settings are fine, but they may be a little on the aggressive side, warning you too much. In any event, checking your browser's security settings is usually a good idea, just in case your browser has a setting you'd like to change. To check security settings in Internet Explorer, click **Tools, Internet Options**, and then the **Security** tab.

If you use a browser other than Internet Explorer, check the browser's help system for information on how to enter your security preferences. All browsers have security features, although they all handle them a little differently.

Points to Remember

- To protect your PC against viruses, purchase and install a good antivirus program, and keep it updated with the latest virus definitions.
- To prevent unauthorized access to your PC, enable the Windows firewall or configure your router's firewall settings.
- Update Windows 7 regularly to ensure that you have the latest security updates installed.
- Log in to a standard user account for your daily activities to limit access to your PC in case a hacker breaks in and takes control of it.
- To avoid potential virus infections from e-mail attachments, install an antivirus program and open attachments only from trusted sources

www.ingramcontent.com/pod-product-compliance
Lightning Source LLC
Chambersburg PA
CBHW080447110426
42743CB00016B/3312